MW01077022

Ravished Armenia

The story of

Aurora Mardiganian

The Christian Girl,
Who Survived the Great Massacres

Interpreted by
Henry L. Gates

With a foreword by
Nora Waln

© Kingfield Press, Inc., New York 1918

© Ararat, Paris, 2019, for this reprint

ISBN: 978-2-9565951-2-0

ararat.editions@gmail.com

All profits from the sale of the book are donated
to actions in favor of Armenia and its diaspora

My dedication

TO each mother and father, in this beautiful land of the United States, who has taught a daughter to believe in God, I dedicate my book.

I saw my own mother's body, its life ebbed out, flung onto the desert because she had taught me that Jesus Christ was my Saviour.

I saw my father die in pain because he said to me, his little girl, "Trust in the Lord; His will be done."

I saw thousands upon thousands of beloved daughters of gentle mothers die under the whip, or the knife, or from the torture of hunger and thirst, or carried away into slavery because they would not renounce the glorious crown of their Christianity.

God saved me that I might bring to America a message from those of my people who are left, and every father and mother will understand that what I tell in these pages is told with love and thankfulness to Him for my escape.

Aurora MARDIGANIAN
The Latham,
New York City,
December, 1918.

Acknowledgment

For verification of these amazing things, which little Aurora told me that I might tell them, in our own language, to all the world, I am indebted to Lord Bryce, formerly British Ambassador to the United States, who was commissioned by the British Government to investigate the massacres; to Dr. Clarence Ussher, of whom Aurora speaks in her story, and who witnessed the massacres at Van; and to Dr. MacCallum, who rescued Aurora at Erzerum and made possible her coming to America. You may read Aurora's story with entire confidence — every word is true. As the story of what happened to one Christian girl, it is a proven document.

H. L. GATES

Foreword

She stood beside me — a slight little girl with glossy black hair. Until I spoke to her and she lifted her eyes in which were written the indelible story of her suffering, I could not believe that she was Aurora Mardiganian whom I had been expecting. She could not speak English, but in Armenian she spoke a few words of greeting.

It was our first meeting and in the spring of last year. Several weeks earlier a letter had come to me telling me about this little Armenian girl who was to be expected, asking me to help her upon her arrival. The year before an Armenian boy had come from our relief station in the Caucasus and kind friends had made it possible to send him to boarding school. I had formed a similar plan to send Aurora to the same school when she should arrive. We talked about education that afternoon, through her interpreter, but she shook her head sadly. She would like to go to school, and study music as her father had planned she should before the massacres, but now she had a message to deliver — a message from her suffering nation to the mothers and fathers of the United States. The determination in the child's eyes made me ask her her age and she answered "Seventeen."

Tired, and worn out nervously, as she was, Aurora insisted upon telling us of the scenes she had left behind her — massacres, families driven out across the desert, girls sold into Turkish harems, women ravished by the roadside, little children dying of starvation. She begged us to help her to help her people. "My father said America was the friend of the oppressed. General Andranik sent me here because he trusted you to help me," she pleaded.

And so her story was translated. Sometimes there had to be intervals of rest of several days, because her suffering had so

7

unnerved her. She wanted to keep at it during all the heat of the summer, but by using the argument that she would learn English, we persuaded her to go to a camp off the coast of Connecticut for three weeks.

You who read the story of Aurora Mardiganian's last three years, will find it hard to believe that in our day and generation such things are possible. Your emotions will doubtless be similar to mine when I first heard of the suffering of her people. I remember very distinctly my feelings, when, early in October of 1917, I attended a luncheon given by the Executive Committee of the American Committee for Armenian and Syrian Relief, to a group of seventeen American Consuls and missionaries who had just returned from Turkey after witnessing two years of massacre and deportation. I listened to persons, the truthfulness of whose statements I could not doubt, tell how a church had been filled with Christian Armenians, women and children, saturated with oil and set on fire, of refined, educated girls, from homes as good as yours or mine, sold in the slave markets of the East, of little children starving to death, and then to the plea for help for the pitiful survivors who have been gathered into temporary relief stations.

I listened almost unable to believe and yet as I looked around the luncheon table there were familiar faces, the faces of men and women whose word I could not doubt — Dr. James L. Barton, Chairman of the American Committee for Armenian and Syrian Relief, Ambassadors **Morgenthau and Elkus,** who spoke from personal knowledge, Cleveland H. Dodge, whose daughter, Mrs. Elizabeth Huntington is in Constantinople, and whose son is in Beirut, both helping with relief work, Miss Lucille Foreman of Germantown, C. V. Vickrey, Executive Secretary of the American Committee for Armenian and Syrian Relief, Dr. Samuel T. Dutton of the World Court League, George T. Scott, Presbyterian Board of Foreign Missions, and others.

And you who read this story as interpreted will find it even harder to believe than I did, because you will not have the personal verification of the men and women who can speak with authority that I had at that luncheon. Since then it has happened that nearly every communication from the East — Persia, Russian Caucasus and the Ottoman Empire, has passed through my hands and I know that conditions have not been exaggerated in this book. In this introduction I want to refer you to Lord Bryce's report, to Ambassador Morgenthau's Story, to the recent speeches of Lord Cecil before the British Parliament, and the files of our own State Department, and you will learn that stories similar to this one can be told by any one of the 3.950.000 refugees, the number now estimated to be destitute in the Near East[1].

This is a human living document. Miss Mardiganian's names, dates and places, do not correspond exactly with similar references to these places made by Ambassador Morgenthau, Lord Bryce and others, but we must take into consideration that she is only a girl of seventeen, that she has lived through one of the most tragic periods of history in that section of the world which has suffered most from the war, that she is not a historian, that her interpreter in giving this story to the American public has not attempted to write a history. He has simply aimed to give her message to the American people that they may understand something of the situation in the Near East during the past years, and help to establish there for the future, a sane and stable government.

Speaking of the character of the Armenians, Ambassador Morgenthau says in a recent article published in the New York *Evening Sun*: "From the times of Herodotus this portion of Asia has borne the name of Armenia. The Armenians of the present day are the direct descendants of the people who inhabited the country 3,000 years ago. Their origin is so ancient that it is lost in fable and mystery. There are still undeciphered cuneiform inscriptions on the rocky hills of Van, the largest Armenian city, that have led certain scholars — though not many, I must admit — to identify the Armenian race with the Hittites of the Bible. What is definitely known about the Armenians, however, is that for ages they have constituted the most civilized and most industrious race in the Eastern section of the Ottoman Empire. From their mountains they have spread over the Sultan's dominions, and form a

---

[1] This number shall include the total number of refugees including Greeks, Assyrians and other wartime refugees.

considerable element in the population of all the large cities. Everywhere they are known for their industry, their intelligence and their decent and orderly lives. They are so superior to the Turks intellectually and morally that much of the business and industry has passed into their hands. With the Greeks, the Armenians constituted the economic strength of the Empire. These people became Christians in the fourth century and established the Armenian Church as their state religion. This is said to be the oldest Christian Church in existence.

"In face of persecutions which have had no parallel elsewhere, these people have clung to their early Christian faith with the utmost tenacity. For 1,500 years they have lived there in Armenia, a little island of Christians, surrounded by backward peoples of hostile religion and hostile race. Their long existence has been one unending martyrdom. The territory which they inhabit forms the connecting link between Europe and Asia, and all the Asiatic invasions — Saracens, Tartars, Mongols, Kurds and Turks — have passed over their peaceful country."

Aurora Mardiganian has come to America to tell the story of her suffering peoples and to do her part in making it possible for her country to be rebuilt. She is only a little girl, but in giving her story to the American people through the daily newspapers, in this book, and the motion picture which is being prepared for that purpose by the American Committee for Armenian and Syrian Relief, she is, I feel, playing one of the greatest parts in helping to reestablish again "peace on earth, good will to men" in ancient Bible Lands, the home in her generation of her people. Her mother, her father, her brothers and sisters are gone, but according to the most careful estimates, 3.950.000 destitute peoples, mostly women and children who had been driven many of them as far as one thousand miles from home, turn their pitiful faces toward America for help in the reconstructive period in which we are now living.

Dr. James L. Barton, who is leaving this month with a commission of two hundred men and women for the purpose of helping to rehabilitate these lands from which Aurora came, is a part of the answer to the call for help from these destitute people. The American Committee for Armenian and Syrian Relief

10

Campaign for $30,000,000, in which it is hoped all of the people of America will participate, is another part of the answer.

You who read this book can play a part also in helping Aurora to deliver her message, by passing it on to someone else when you have finished with it.

Nora WALN
Publicity Secretary,
American Committee for
Armenian and Syrian Relief
December 2, 1918
One Madison Ave., New York

ARSHALUS - THE LIGHT OF THE MORNING

A PROLOGUE TO THE STORY

OLD VARTABED, the shepherd whose flocks had clothed three generations, stood silhouetted against the skies on the summit of a Taurus hill. His figure was motionless, erect and very tall. The signs of age were in every crease of his grave, strong face, yet his hands folded loosely on his stick, for he would have scorned to lean upon it.

To the east and north spread the plains of the Mamuret-ul-Aziz, with here and there a plateau reaching out from a nest of foothills. Each Spring, through twenty-five centuries, other shepherds than Old Vartabed had stood on this same hilltop to watch the plains and plateaux of the Mamuret-ul-Aziz turn green, but few had seen the grass and shrubs sprout so early as they had this year. Old Vartabed should have been greatly pleased at such promise of a good season, and should have spoken to his sheep about it — for that was his way.

But the shepherd was troubled. A strange foreboding had come to him in the night. Even at daybreak he could not shake it off. He was gazing now, not at the stretches of welcome green which soon would soothe the bleating of his sheep, but across into the north beyond, where the blue line of the Euphrates was lost in the haze of dawn. What his old eyes sought there, he did not know; but something seemed to threaten from up there in the north.

Suddenly the lazy, droning call to the Third Prayer, with which the devout Mohammedan greets the light of day, floated up from the valley at Old Vartabed's feet. It brought the shepherd out of his reverie abruptly. "There, that was it! That was the sign. The danger might come from the north, but it would show itself first, whatever it was to be, in the city."

The shepherd looked down into the valley, onto the housetops and the narrow, winding streets that separated them. He caught the glint of the minaret as the muezzin again intoned his summons. Quickly his eyes leaped across the city to where the first glimpse of sunshine played about a crumbled pile of brown and gray — the ruins of the castle of Tchemesh, an ancient Armenian king. A piteous sadness gathered in his face. The minaret still stood; the castle of the king was fallen. That was why there were two sets of prayers in the city, and why trouble was coming out of the north.

The old man planted his stick upright in the ground as a sign to his sheep that where the stick stood their shepherd was bound to return. Then he picked his way down the path that led to the lower slopes where the houses of the city began. With a firm, even step that belied his many years, he strode through the city until he came to the streets marked by the imposing homes of the rich. A short turn along the side of the park that served as a public square brought him to the home of the banker, Mardiganian. In this house Old Vartabed was always welcome. He had been the keeper of herds belonging to three succeeding heads of the Mardiganian families.

A servant woman opened the door in the street wall and admitted the shepherd to the inner garden. When she had closed the door again, the visitor asked:

"Is the Master still within the house, or has he gone this early to his business?"

"Shame upon you for the asking!" the woman replied, with a servant's quick uncivility to her kind. "Have you forgotten what day it is, that you should think the Master would be at business?"

Amazement showed in the old man's eyes. The woman saw that he had, indeed, forgotten. She spoke more kindly:

"Do you not know, Vartabed, that this is Easter Sunday morning?"

The old man accepted the reminder, but his dignity quickly reasserted itself. "If you live as many days as Old Vartabed you will wish to forget more than one of them — perhaps one that is coming soon more than any other."

The woman had no patience for the sententiousness of age, and the veiled threat of coming ill she put down for petulance. But her sharp reply fell upon unheeding ears. The shepherd crossed the garden without further parleys and entered the house.

The house of the Mardiganians was typical of the homes of the well-to-do Armenians of to-day. The wide doorway which opened from the garden was approached by handsome steps of white marble, and the spacious hall within was floored with large slabs of the same material. Outside, the house presented a rather gloomy appearance, because, perhaps, of the need of protection against the sometimes rigorous climate; inside there was every sign of luxury and opulence. The space of ground occupied was prodigious, as the rooms were terraced, one above the other, the roof of one being used as a dooryard garden for the one above.

In the large reception room, into which Old Vartabed strode, there was a great stone fireplace, with a low divan branching out on either side and running around three sides of the room. Beautiful tapestry covers of native manufacture, and silk cushions made by hand, covered this divan. Soft, thick rugs of tekke, which is a Persian and Kurdish weave built upon felt foundations, were strewn over the marble floor. Over the fireplace hung a rare Madonna; a landscape by a popular Armenian artist, and a Dutch harbor by Peniers hung on the walls at the side. In a corner of the room, under a floor lamp, was a piano. Oriental delight in bright colorings was apparent, but the ensemble was tasteful and subdued.

The shepherd waited, standing, in the center of the room until his employer entered and gave him the Easter morning greeting which Armenia has preserved since the world was young:

"Christ is risen from the dead, my good Vartabed!"

"Blessed be the resurrection of Christ" the old man replied, as the custom dictates. Then he spoke, with an earnestness which the other man quickly detected, of that which had brought him to the house.

It was a vision he had seen during the night. "Our Saint Gregory appeared to me in my sleep and pressed his hand upon me

15

heavily. 'Awake, Old Vartabed; awake! Thy sheep are in danger, even though they be favored of God. Awake and save them!' This, the good saint said to me. Hurriedly I arose, but when my old eyes were fully opened the vision was gone. I rushed out to the fold, but it was only I who disturbed the flock. They were resting peacefully.

"But I could not sleep again. Each time my eyes closed our Saint stood before me, seeming to reprove my idleness. At dawn I took my sheep to the hills — and then I remembered!"

Here the shepherd hesitated. He had spoken fast, and was nearly breathless. His employer had listened with the consideration due to one so old, and so faithful, but not without a trace of amusement in his immobile face.

"It is a pity, Vartabed, your sleep was restless. This morning, of all others, you should be joyful. Tell me what it was you remembered at dawn, and then dismiss it from your mind."

"Some things, Master, neither you nor I can dismiss from our minds. I remembered that once before our Saint appeared to me in my sleep with a warning of danger. I gave no attention then, for I was younger, and thoughtless. Those, also, were joyous times in Armenia, for there was peace and prosperity. But that very day the holocaust came out of the north; for that was twenty years ago."

Now, the other man started. He was shaken by a convulsive shudder, and his face blanched. Twenty years ago — that was when two hundred thousand of his people were massacred by Abdul Hamid! Without a word he walked to a window, separated the curtains and looked out upon the house garden.

The banker, Mardiganian, was a true type of the successful, modern Armenian business man. He did not often smile, but his voice was kind, and his eyes were gentle. In the Easter morning promenades in any avenue in Europe or America he would have been a conventional figure, passed without notice. When he turned from the window, after a moment, only a close observer could have detected in his face or manner that inexplicable, intangible something which, indelibly, marks a race cradled in oppression.

"What happened twenty years ago, my Vartabed, can never happen again. We Armenians have done nothing to rouse the anger of our over-lords, the Turks. On the contrary, we have proven our willingness to serve the state. Our young men have been called into this great war which is ravaging the world. Even though their sympathies are with the Sultan's enemies, they have not shown it. They have freely given their lives in battle for a cause they hate, that the Turk may have no excuse to vent his wrath upon our people. Less than a week ago the Sultan's minister, the powerful Enver, expressed his gratitude to us for the services we are rendering the Crescent. They dare not molest us again."

"But the vision that came to me last night was the same that would have warned me that night in 1895 of the tragedy then in store for us."

"This time, nevertheless, it was but an idle dream."

The banker spoke with the finality of conviction. The shepherd was affronted by his calm disbelief in the sign of coming evil, as the shepherd considered it. The old man left the room and crossed the garden in high dudgeon. His hand was upon the gate, and in another moment he would have been gone when a fresh, youthful voice arrested him.

"Vartabed — wait; I am coming!"

The old man stopped abruptly. Looking back he saw coming toward him the one who was closer to his heart than any other living thing — Arshalus, a daughter of the Mardiganians.

Arshalus — that means "The Light of the Morning." There is but one word in America into which the Armenian name can be translated — "The Aurora." And no other would be so fitting. She was a merry-eyed child of fourteen years, hair and eyes as black as night; smile and spirit as sunny as the brightest day. Every sheep in Old Vartabed's flock was her pet, especially the black ones.

When she reached the waiting shepherd Aurora quickly discovered that he was glum, and she chose to be piqued about it.

"Surely you were not going without wishing me the happiness of the Easter time, or has Old Vartabed ceased to care for the one who plagues him so much?" She made a great show of pouting, but the old man's hurt could not be so easily mended. Perhaps the sight of Aurora intensified it.

"It is idle to wish happiness; it is better to give it. When one has none to give, he has no mission. I have no joy to give to-day, even to you, my Aurora, and so I had not thought of seeking you."

"That is very wrong, Vartabed. Today Christ is risen, and there is joy everywhere. And even more for me than many others. Just yesterday my father told me that before another Easter comes, I am to go away to finish my schooling — to Constantinople, or, perhaps, to Switzerland or Paris. Does that not make you happy for me, Vartabed?"

For an instant the old man gazed down upon the upturned face. Then his hand reached for the gate again, as if to give support to the tall, straight body that seemed to droop. Aurora thought she had pained him. With an impulsive fondness she raised her hands as if to rest them upon the old man's breast. But before she could reach him the shepherd was gone, and the gate had closed between them.

An hour later Old Vartabed again stood on the summit of the hill, looking down upon the city and the plains of the Mamuret-ul-Aziz, bathed, now, in the glory of the full morning sun. A few miles to the south lay the ridges and long abandoned tunnels which, according to tradition, once were the busy workings of Solomon's mines. Harpout, where the caravans stop; Van, the metropolis, and Sivas, the "City of Hope," were far beyond the horizon, outpost cities of a nation which was born before history. The old man's thoughts visited each of these jewel cities in turn, and pictured the hope and faith with which they celebrated the coming of Easter. Then he turned again to the spires and housetops reaching up from the plains below. For he was thinking not only of Armenia — the beautiful, golden Armenia of that Easter day in 1915, but, also, of the child who was named for "The Light of the Morning."

H. L. GATES

18

I

WHEN THE PASHA CAME TO MY HOUSE

MY story begins with Easter Sunday morning, in April, 1915. In my father's house we prepared to observe the day with a joyous reverence, increased by the news from Constantinople that the Turkish government recently had expressed its gratitude for the loyal and valuable service of the Armenian troops in the Great War. When Turkey joined in the war, almost six months before, a great fear spread throughout Armenia. Without the protecting influence of France and England, my people were anxious lest the Turks take advantage of their opportunity and begin again the old oppression of their Christian subjects. The young Armenian men would have preferred to fight with the Sultan's enemies, but they hurried to enlist in the Ottoman armies, to prove they were not disloyal.

And now that the Sultan had acknowledged their sacrifices, the fear of new persecutions at the hands of our Moslem rulers gradually had disappeared.

And in all our city, Tchemesh-Gedzak, twenty miles north of Harpout, the capital of the district of Mamuret-ul-Aziz, there was none more grateful for the promise of continued peace in Armenia than my father and mother, and Lusanne, my elder sister and I. I was only fourteen years old, and Lusanne was not yet seventeen, but even little girls are always afraid in Armenia. I was quite excited that morning over my father's Easter gift to me — his promise that soon I could go to a European school and finish my education as befits a banker's daughter. Lusanne was to be married, and she was bent upon enjoying the last Easter day of her maidenhood. Even the early visit that morning of Old Vartabed, our shepherd, who came just after daybreak, with a prophecy of trouble, did not dampen our spirits.

Standing before my looking glass I was rearranging for the hundredth time the blue ribbons with which I had dressed my hair with, I must confess, a secret hope that they would be the envy of all the other girls at the church service. Lusanne was making use of her elder sister's privilege to scold me heartily for my vanity. Lusanne was always very prim, and quiet. I was just about to tell her that she was only jealous because she soon would be a wife and forbidden to wear blue ribbons any more, when my mother came into the room. She stopped just inside the door, and leaned against the wall. She did not say a word — just looked at me.

"Mother, what is it?" I cried. She did not answer, but silently pointed to the window. Lusanne and I ran at once to look down into the street. There at the gate to our yard stood three Turkish gendarmes, each with a rifle, rigidly on guard. On their arms was the band that marked them as personal attendants of Husein Pasha, the military commandant in our district.

I turned to my mother for an explanation. She had fallen in a heap on the floor and was weeping. She did not speak, but pointed downward and I knew that Husein Pasha had come to our house, and was downstairs. Then my happiness was gone, and I, too, fell to the floor and cried. Somehow I felt that the end had come.

For a long time the powerful Husein Pasha, who was very rich and a friend of the Sultan himself, had wanted me for his harem. His big house sat in the midst of beautiful gardens, just outside the city. There he had gathered more than a dozen of the prettiest Christian girls from the surrounding towns. In Armenia the Mutassarif, or Turkish commandant, is an official of great power. He accepts no orders, except those that come direct from the Sultan's ministers, and, as a rule, he is cruel and autocratic.

It is dangerous for an Armenian father to displease the Mutassarif. When this representative of the Sultan sees a pretty Armenian girl, he would like to add to his harem there are many ways he may go about getting her. The way of Husein Pasha was to bluntly ask her father to sell or give her to him, with a veiled threat that if the father refused, he would be persecuted. To make the sale of the girl legal and give the Mutassarif the right to make her his concubine it was necessary only for him to persuade or compel her to forswear Christ and become Mohammedan.

Three times Husein Pasha had asked my father to give me to him. Three times my father had defied his anger and refused. The Pasha was afraid to punish us, as my father was wealthy, and through his friendship with the British Consul at Harpout, Mr. Stevens, had obtained protection of the Vali, or Governor, of the Mamuret-ul-Aziz province. But now the British Consul was gone. The Vali was afraid of no one. And Husein Pasha could, I knew, do as he pleased. Instinctively I knew, too, that his visit to our house, with his escort of armed soldiers, meant that he had come again to ask for me.

I clung to my mother and Lusanne, with my two younger sisters holding onto my skirt, while we listened at the head of the stairs to my father and the governor talking. Husein was no longer asking for me — he was demanding. I heard him say: "Soon orders from Constantinople will arrive; you Christian dogs are to be sent away; not a man, woman or child who denies Mohammed will be permitted to remain. When that time comes there is none to save you but me. Give me the girl Aurora, and I will take all your family under my protection until the crisis is past. Refuse and you know what you may expect!"

My father could not speak aloud. He was choked with fear and horror. My mother screamed. I begged mother to let me rush downstairs and give myself to the Pasha. I would do anything to save her and father and my little brothers and sisters. Then father found his voice, and we heard him saying to the Pasha:

"God's will shall be done — and He would never will that my child should sacrifice herself to save us."

My mother held me closer. "Your father has spoken — for you and us."

Husein Pasha went away in anger, his escort marching stiffly behind. Scarcely had he disappeared than there was a great commotion in the streets. Crowds began to assemble at the corners.

Men ran to our house to tell us news that had just been brought by a horseman who had ridden in wild haste from Harpout.

"They are massacring at Van; men, women and children are being hacked to pieces. The Kurds are stealing the girls!"

Van is the greatest city in Armenia. It was once the capital of the Vannic kingdom of Queen Semiramis. It was the home of Xerxes, and, we are taught, was built by the King Aram in the midst of what was the first land uncovered after the Deluge — the Holy Place where the ark of Noah rested. It is very dear to Armenians, and was one of the centers of our church and national life. It lies two hundred miles away from Tchemesh-Gedzak, and was the home of more than 50,000 of our people. The Vali of Van, Djevdet Bey, was the principal Turkish ruler in Armenia — and the most cruel. A massacre at Van meant that soon it would spread over all Armenia.

They brought the horseman from Harpout to our house. My father tried to question him but all he could say was:

"Ermenleri hep kesdiler — hep gitdi bitdi!" — "The Armenians all killed — all gone, all dead!" He moaned it over and over. In Harpout the news had come by telegraph, and the horseman who belonged in our city had ridden at once to warn us.

I begged my father and mother to let me run at once to the palace of Husein Pasha and tell him I would do whatever he wished if he would save my family before orders came to disturb us. But mother held me close, while father would only say, "God's will be done, and that would not be it."

Lusanne was crying. Little Aruciag and Sarah, my younger sisters, were crying, too. My father was very pale and his hands trembled when he put them on my shoulders and tried to comfort me. I closed my eyes and seemed to see my father and mother and sisters and brothers, all lying dead in the massacre I feared would come, sooner or later. And Husein Pasha had said I could save them! But I couldn't disobey my father. Suddenly I thought of Father Rhoupen.

I broke away from my mother and ran out of the house, through the back entrance and into the street that led to the church where Father Rhoupen was waiting for his congregation. No one

22

had had the courage to tell the holy man of the news from Van. When I ran into the little room behind the altar, he was wondering why his people had not come.

I fell at his feet, and it was a long time before I could stop my tears long enough to tell him why I was there. But he knew something had happened. He stroked my hair, and waited. When I could speak I told him of the visit of Husein Pasha, and what he said to us — and then I told him of the message the horseman had brought. I pleaded with him to tell me that it would be right for me to send word to Husein Pasha that I would be his willing concubine if he would only save my parents and my brothers and sisters.

Father Rhoupen made me tell it twice. When I had finished the second time, he put a hand on my head and said, "Let us ask God, my child!"

Then Father Rhoupen prayed.

He asked God to guide me in the way I should go. I do not remember all the prayer, for I was crying too bitterly and was too frightened, but I know the priest pleaded for me and my people, and that he reminded the Father we were His first believers and had been true to Him through many centuries of persecution. As the priest went on, I became soothed, and unconsciously I began to listen — hoping to hear with my own ears the answer I felt must surely come down from up above to Father Rhoupen's plea.

When he said "Amen" the priest knelt with me, and together we waited. Suddenly Father Rhoupen pressed me close to his breast and began to speak.

"The way is clear, my child. The answer has come. Trust in Jesus Christ and He will save you as He deems best. It were better that you should die, if need be, or suffer even worse than death, than by your example lead others to forswear their faith in the Saviour. Go back to your father and mother and comfort them, but obey them."

All that day and the next, messengers rode back and forth between Harpout and our city, bringing the latest scraps of news from Van. We were filled with joy when we heard the Armenians had barricaded themselves and were fighting back, but we dreaded the consequences. No one slept that night in our city. All day and all night Father Rhoupen and his assistant priests and religious teachers in the Christian College went from house to house to pray with family groups.

The principal men in the city waited on Husein Pasha to ask him if we were in danger. He told them their fears were groundless, that the trouble at Van was merely a riot. My father and mother clutched eagerly at this half promise of security, but Tuesday we knew we had been deceived. That morning Husein Pasha ordered the doors of the district jail opened, and the criminals — bandits and murderers — who were confined there, released and brought to his palace.

An hour later each one of these outlaws had been dressed in the uniform of the gendarmes, given a rifle, a bayonet and a long dagger and lined up in the public square to await orders. That is the Turkish way when there is bad work to do.

At noon officers of the gendarmes, or, as they are called, zaptiehs, rode through the city posting notices on the walls and fences at every street corner. My father had gone to Harpout early in the morning to confer with rich Armenian bankers there and to appeal direct to Ismail Bey, the Vali. Mother was too weak from worry to go to the corner and read the notices, so Lusanne and I went at once. The paper read:

ARMENIANS

You are hereby commanded by His Excellency, Husein Pasha, to immediately go into your houses and remain within doors until it is the pleasure of His Excellency to again permit you to go about your affairs. All Armenians found upon the streets, at their places of business or otherwise absent from their homes, later than one hour after noon of this day will be arrested and severely punished.

ALI AGHAZADE, *Mayor*

When we reported to our mother she was greatly worried because of our father's absence at Harpout. He might ride into the city at any time during the afternoon, ignorant of the orders, and be caught

24

in the streets. Our brother Paul, who was fifteen years old, was visiting at a neighbor's. We sent him, through narrow, back streets, out of the city and onto the plains where he could watch the road our father must ride along, and, should he appear before dark, warn him of the order. We had reason later to be thankful father was away.

We could not imagine what the order meant. We could not bring ourselves to believe it meant a deliberate massacre was planned, and that this means was taken to have us all in our homes for the convenience of the zaptiehs.

At 4 o'clock, gendarmes, among them the prisoners released from jail, marched up to the homes of the wealthiest men, with orders for them to attend an audience with Husein Pasha.

When mother explained to the officer who came to our door that my father was out of town the zaptiehs searched the house, roughly pushing my mother aside when she got in their way. They then demanded the keys to my father's business place. When Lusanne ran upstairs to get them the officer insisted upon going with her. While she was getting the keys from my father's room, he embraced her, tearing open her dress as he did so. When she screamed, he slapped her in the face so hard she fell onto the floor. He left her there and went out with his men.

From our windows we could overlook the public square. Here the zaptiehs gathered fifty of the city's leading men. Among them were Father Rhoupen; the president of the Christian College, which had been founded by American missionaries; several professors and physicians; bankers, the principal merchants and other business men.

Instead of marching their prisoners toward the palace of the Pasha, the guards turned them toward the other part of the city. Then we knew they were being taken, not to an audience with the commandant, but to the jail which had been emptied by the Mutassarif that morning.

Many women, when they realized where their husbands were being taken, ignored the order to keep to their homes, ran into the street and tried to rush up to their men folk. The gendarmes knocked them aside with rifle butts. One woman, the wife of a

25

professor, managed to break through the guard and reach her husband. A gendarme tried to pull her away, but she clung tightly, screaming. The soldier turned his rifle about and drove his bayonet into her. Her husband leaped at the man's throat and was killed by another gendarme.

The prisoners were compelled to march over the bodies of the professor and his wife, while their children, who had also run out of their house, stood aside, wringing their hands and weeping, until the company passed, when they were permitted to tug the bodies of their parents into their home. None of us who watched dared go to the assistance of these little ones.

The jail is a rambling stone building, built more than seven centuries ago. Originally it was a monastery, but the Turks took possession of it in 1580, and have used it as a prison ever since. It is surrounded by a high wall and has a large courtyard onto which the great, barren dungeons open.

Throughout that afternoon mother, Lusanne and I waited anxiously for father to come from Harpout. Toward evening a gendarme came to the house and asked if father had returned yet, saying that he was missed "at the audience with the Mutassarif." Mother asked him why the men folk were taken to jail, if the Mutassarif wanted to see them. The soldier said the governor thought that would be handier, as it was a long walk to the palace. We were comforted a little by that explanation, but when evening came and the men had not returned to their homes, we became worried again. And we began to fear, too, that father and Paul had been intercepted. At dark the wives and daughters of the men who had been taken from their homes could not stand the suspense any longer. Braving the order to remain indoors they began to gather in the streets, and little companies of women and children, and even the more daring men, moved toward the jails. They waited outside until well toward midnight, hoping to catch a glimpse of their relatives or to hear what was going on inside. At 11 o'clock, the prison gates opened and Husein Pasha, in his carriage and escorted by a heavy guard of mounted soldiers, came out.

The women crowded around him, but the soldiers drove them away. Scarcely had the Pasha's carriage disappeared than there was

26

shouting and screaming in the prison. Lusanne and I, who had stolen up to the prison wall, ran home frightened. Father and Paul were there, having reached home late in the evening.

Father looked very careworn. He took me into his arms and kissed me in a strange way. Big tears were in his eyes when I looked into them. I knew, without asking, that he had not succeeded in his mission to Harpout for protection. We sat up all that night, listening to the cries that came from the prison. We learned the next day what had happened, when the one man who had escaped crept into his home to be hidden.

When Husein Pasha arrived at the prison he told the men who had been gathered that new word had come from Constantinople that the Armenians were not loyal to Turkey, and that they had been plotting to help the Allies. He demanded that the prisoners tell him what they knew of such plots. Every one of them assured him there had been no such plotting, that the Armenians wanted only to live in peace with their Turkish neighbors, obey the Sultan and do him whatever service was demanded of them. Husein seemed at last convinced and went away, saying the men could all return to their homes in the morning.

While the prisoners were congratulating each other upon their promised release, and hoping there might be some way to get word to their families in the meantime, gendarmes appeared and drove the men into one corner of the courtyard. While the others were held back by the levelled guns and bayonets one prisoner at a time was pulled into a ring of soldiers and ordered to confess that he had been conspiring against the Sultan.

As each one denied the accusation and declared he would confess to nothing, he was stripped of his clothes and the gendarmes fell to beating him on his naked back with leather thongs. As fast as the men fainted from the lashing, they were thrown to one side until they revived, when they were beaten again, until all the soldiers had taken turns with the thongs and were tired. Eight of the older men died under the beatings. Their bodies were thrown into a corner of the jail yard.

While they were beating Father Rhoupen an officer interfered. He said it was a waste of time to beat the priest, as all priests must

27

be killed anyway. He then turned to Father Rhoupen and told him he could live only if he would forswear Christ and become Mohammedan. If he refused, the officer said, he would be beaten until he died.

Poor Father Rhoupen was almost too weak to answer. When the soldiers dropped him, at the officer's command, he fell into a heap on the ground. When he tried to speak his head shook and the Turk thought he was signifying he would accept Mohammed.

"Hold him up — on his feet," the officer ordered.

Two soldiers lifted him. The officer commanded him to repeat the creed of Islam — "There is only one God, and Mohammed is his prophet."

"There is only one God" — Father Rhoupen began, just as clearly as he could, and with his eyes turned full upon the cruel officer. He stopped for breath, and then went on — "and Jesus Christ, His Son, is my Saviour!"

The officer drew his sword and cut off Father Rhoupen's head.

Professor Poladian, president of the College, was next told that he might save his life if he would profess Mohammed. Professor Poladian was one of the most loved men in all Armenia. He had studied at Yale University, in the United States, and had been highly honored by England and France because of his noble deeds. He was very old.

I loved him more than any man besides my father, because once when I was very little, I was sick and cried when I had to stay away from a Christmas tree at the College on which Professor Poladian had hung bags of candy for all the little girls of Tchemesh-Gedzak. Professor Poladian asked Lusanne, my sister, why I was not with the other children who gathered about the tree, and when she told him I was at home, ill, and that I cried because I couldn't come, he drove all the way to our house, almost two miles, brought me my candy bag and told me the Christmas story of the birth of Christ. I remember after that I always wanted to pray to Professor Poladian after I had prayed to God, until my mother made me understand why I shouldn't.

Professor Poladian was not beaten, but the officer told him he had been spared only that he might swear faith in Islam. The

Professor was almost overcome with his suffering at having to witness the treatment of his friends, but he told the officer he would give his life rather than deny his religion. The soldiers then tore out his finger nails, one by one, and his toe nails and pulled out his hair and beard, and then stabbed him with knives until he died.

Throughout the night, the screams from the prison yard continued, and the women waiting outside were frantic. At dawn, soldiers drove the women away, telling them their husbands would soon be home.

As soon as the women were out of sight, the soldiers took out the men who had lived through the torture and, tying them together with a long rope, marched them out of the city behind the jail toward the Murad River, ten miles away. When they reached the river bank the soldiers set upon the men and stabbed them to death with bayonets. Only the one escaped by pulling a dead body on top of him and making believe that he, too, was dead.

The next day, Thursday, which is the day before the Mohammedan Sunday, the soldiers went through the streets at 9 o'clock, calling for all Armenian men over eighteen years of age, to assemble in the public square. In every street an officer stopped at house doors and told the people that any man over eighteen who was not in the square in one hour would be killed.

Mother and Lusanne and I flew to father's arms. We each tried to get our arms around his neck. He was very sad and quiet. "One at a time, my dear ones," he said, and made us wait while he kissed and said good-by to each of us in turn. Little Sarah, who was seven, and Hovnan, who was six, he held in his arms a long time. Then he kissed me on the lips, such as he had never done before. He told mother she must not cry, but be very brave. Then he went out.

Little Paul followed father at a distance, to be near him as long as possible. When father got to the square Paul tried to turn back, but a soldier saw him and caught him by the collar, saying, "You go along, too, then we won't have to gather you up with the women to-morrow." Father protested that Paul was only fifteen, but the soldiers wouldn't listen. So my brother never came back home.

29

II

THE DAYS OF TERROR BEGIN

I HAD gone upstairs to my window to watch father crossing the street to the square. Mother had fallen onto a divan in the reception room downstairs. Lusanne and my little brothers and sisters stayed with her, even the little ones trying to make believe that, perhaps, father would return. When I saw the soldier take Paul, too, I screamed. Mother heard and came running upstairs, Lusanne and the others following. I was the only one who had seen. I would have to tell them — to tell them that not only father, but that little Paul, who had wanted to be a priest, when he grew up, like Father Rhoupen, was gone too. For a moment I could not speak. Mother thought something had happened to father in the street, and that I had seen.

"Tell me quick — what is it? Have they killed him?" she cried. I couldn't answer — except to shake my head. Suddenly mother missed Paul for the first time. Something must have told her. She asked Lusanne: "Where is my boy? Where is Paul? Why isn't he here?"

Lusanne started to run downstairs to look in the yard. I motioned her not to go. I put my arms around mother and said, between my sobs:

"They took Paul too — he is with our father!"

Mother sank upon the floor and buried her face. Lusanne and I knelt beside her. But she didn't cry. Her eyes were dry when she gathered us to her. I never saw my mother cry after that, even when the Turkish soldiers, at the orders of Ahmed Bey, were beating her to death while they made me look on before returning me to Ahmed's harem.

Out of my window we could see the men comforting each other, or talking excitedly with the leaders, in the square. By the middle of the afternoon more than 3,000 men and older boys had assembled. The soldiers and zaptiehs searched our houses that no man over eighteen might escape. When women clung to husbands and fathers the soldiers said the men were summoned only to be addressed by Ishmail Bey, the Vali, who was coming up from his capital, Harpout. Some of the women believed this explanation. Others knew it was not true.

Not very far from our house was the home of Andranik, a young man who had graduated from the American School at Marsovan, and who had come to our city with his parents to teach in our schools. He was very popular in the city, and it was to him Lusanne was to be married. When the Turks conscripted young Armenian men, they spared Andranik because of his position as a teacher.

When his father answered the summons to the square, Andranik remained behind. He disguised himself in a dress belonging to his sister and made his way to the edge of the city where he bought a horse from a Turk whom he knew he could trust. By the Turk, Andranik sent word to Lusanne that he would ride to Harpout, where he knew the German Consul-General, Count Wolf von Wolfskehl, and beg of this powerful German official to intercede for the Armenians of Tchemesh-Gedzak.

Lusanne was much encouraged when she heard Andranik was safe. All afternoon neighboring women, some of them wives of wealthy men, came to our house to look from our windows into the square, hoping to catch a glimpse of their loved ones. The soldiers would not let the women gather near the square, nor communicate with the men.

One pretty woman, Mrs. Sirpouhi, who had been married not quite a year to a son of our richest manufacturer, was just about to become a mother. From our window she caught sight of her husband. She could not keep herself from running across to the square, screaming as she went, "My Vartan — my Vartan!" Vartan was his name.

The young husband heard his wife calling and ran to the edge of the square, holding out his arms to her. Just as she was about to throw herself upon him a zaptieh struck her on the head with his gun. When this zaptieh and his companions saw the young woman was almost a mother they took turns running their bayonets into her. The husband fell to the ground. I think he fainted. The soldiers carried him off. They left his bride's body where it fell.

At sundown, when nearly all the Christian women in the city must have cried their eyes dry, as did Lusanne and I, we heard the muezzin calling the First Prayer from the minarets of the El Hasan Mosque in the Mohammedan quarter. It seemed to me the muezzin was mocking us as he sang: "There is no God but Allah; come to prayer; come to security!" Without letting mother know, I knelt by myself and asked our God if He would not think of us — and send our fathers back. Perhaps He heard me for as soon as the Mohammedan prayer was over a soldier came to our door.

He said father had paid him to bring a message; that he would be able to speak to us if we should go at once to the north corner of the square. To prove his message was true the soldier showed us father's ring.

With my little sisters and brothers holding to our hands, mother, Lusanne and I ran quickly to the north corner, and there father and Paul were awaiting us. For a time he could not speak. Then he said:

"We are to be driven into the desert!"

The officers had told them they would be taken only to Arabkir, sixty miles away, and allowed to camp there until the Turks were ready for them to return home again. Father said he hoped this were true — but he did not believe they would be allowed to return. He told mother that since little Paul was along, he would like to have her bring him a blanket to wrap up in at night, and money. He had with him a hundred liras, or $440. in American money, but perhaps if he had more, he thought he could bribe the soldiers to let Paul ride a horse, or perhaps, escape when they began the march.

Mother and I hurried to the house. She went into the basement, where father had hidden a great deal of money for us. When I went to get a blanket, I thought of my "yorgan," a birthday blanket father had brought me from Smyrna when I was ten years old. It was the most beautiful thing I had. The Ten Commandments were woven into it, and it had been made, many people had said, a thousand years ago. I took this to Paul and another blanket for father. Paul cried when he saw I had given him my yorgan. We wrapped dried fruit, and cheese in thin bread, also, to give them. Mother took 200 liras — almost a thousand dollars.

The soldiers would not let us talk long to father the second time. We stood across the street just looking at him until it was too dark to see him anymore, and then we went home. We never saw father or Paul again.

When we reached our house, we found Abdoullah Bey, the police chief, waiting in the parlor. Abdoullah always had been a friend of father's, and we thought him a kindly man. Perhaps he would have helped us if he could, but when mother begged him to have Paul, at least, restored to us, he showed us a written order, signed by Ismail Bey, the Vali, which had been given him by Husein Pasha. It read:

"During the process of deportation of the Armenians if any Moslem resident or visitor from the surrounding country endeavors to conceal or otherwise protect a Christian, first his house shall be burned, then the Christian killed before his eyes, and then the Moslem's family and himself shall be killed."

"You see I cannot help you," Abdoullah Bey said, "even though I would. But I can advise you as a friend. You have two daughters who are young. It is still possible for them to renounce your religion and accept Allah. I will take word personally, if you wish, to Husein Pasha that your Lusanne and Aurora will say the rek'ah (the oath to Mohammed). He is willing to take them both, and thus spare them and you many things, which, perhaps, are about to happen. Soon it may be too late."

Husein wanted us both! I remembered Father Rhoupen's words, "Trust in God and be true to Him." But it seemed as if I

33

ought to sacrifice myself. Even then I would have gone to the Pasha's house, but mother said to Abdoullah:

"Tell the Pasha we belong to God, and will accept whatever He wills!" Abdoullah respected mother for her courage. He bowed to her as he went out. "I am sorry for what may come," he said.

That evening Andranik returned from Harpout and came at once to our house. He still wore his sister's dress. When he appeared at the door Lusanne ran into his arms. I read in his face bad news.

"I begged of Count von Wolfskehl to save us. He said the Sultan had ordered that no Christian subject be left alive in Turkey, and that he thought the Sultan had done right."

Lusanne secretly had thought Andranik would be successful. She had such confidence in him she did not think he could fail. She was overcome when her hope was destroyed, but she thought more of Andranik than of herself. She begged him to try to escape. Andranik decided he would remain in his women's clothes. Lusanne cut off some of her own hair and arranged it on his head so bits of it would show under his shawl and make him look more nearly like a girl. They thought perhaps he might get out of the city at night, unmolested, and hide with friendly farmers.

But, somehow, the authorities learned Andranik had not surrendered himself. Early in the evening the zaptiehs under command of Abdoullah, surrounded his house and demanded that he come out. When his mother said he was not there, the gendarme chief replied that if he did not appear at once the house would be burned with all who were in it.

A neighbor woman ran in to tell us. Andranik threw off his disguise, took an old saber father had hung on our wall, and rushed out. He cut his way through the gendarmes and got into his home, where he found his mother and sister and his other relatives in a panic of fear. The gendarmes shouted to him to come out at once. Andranik saw them bringing up cans of oil. He kissed his mother and sister again and stepped out into the street. They killed him with knives on the doorstep. His sister ran out and threw herself on his body, and they killed her, too. When a neighbor told us what had happened, Lusanne ran out to Andranik's house and helped his mother carry in the two bodies.

Father and the other men were taken away that night. In our house, we were sitting in my room trying to pick them out from the shadows in the square made by the torches and lanterns of the zaptiehs, when many new soldiers appeared, and, suddenly, there was a great shouting. Soon we saw the men, formed into a long line, march out of the square, with zaptiehs and soldiers all about them. It was too dark for us to identify father and Paul, but we knew they would be looking up at our window and hoped they could see us.

They took the men toward the Kara River, which is a branch of the Euphrates. Many were so old and feeble they could not walk so far, and fell to the ground. The zaptiehs killed these with their knives and left their bodies behind. It was daylight when they came to the little village of Gwazim, which is on the river bank twelve miles away. There was a large building at Gwazim which the Turks sometimes used as a barracks when there was war with the Kurds, and at other times as a prison. Half the men were put into this building and told they would have to stay until the next day. The zaptiehs then took the others across the river toward Arabkir.

At noon of that day the zaptiehs returned to Gwazim. They had killed all the men they had taken across the river just as soon as they were out of sight of the village. When we, in Tchemesh-Gedzak, heard that part of our men had been left in the prison, hundreds of women walked the dusty road to Gwazim. Lusanne and I went, hoping to get one more glimpse of father and Paul.

In Gwazim there was an aged Armenian woman who had lived in our city at the time of the massacre in 1895. She was pretty then, and when the Kurds stole her, she saved her life by turning Mohammedan. Then she was sold to a Turkish bey at Gwazim. He kept her in his harem until she grew old. All the time, while professing Islam, she secretly was Christian. The bey had given her the name "Fatimeh."

Fatimeh persuaded the guards at the prison to let her take water to the men. When she told the prisoners the zaptiehs had returned

35

without the other men they knew the same fate was in store for them.

When Fatimeh came out she told me father and Paul were inside and had sent word to us to be hopeful. In a little while we saw her going into the prison again, this time with two big rocks, so heavy she could hardly carry them, hidden in her water buckets. She came out again and filled her buckets with coal oil.

When it was dark the younger men, who were strong and brave, killed all the older men by hitting their heads with the rocks Fatimeh had taken them. Father killed Paul first, because he was so little. When all the old and feeble men were dead, the young men prayed that God would think they had done right in not letting the old men suffer and then they spread the oil, set it afire, and threw themselves in the flames. Fatimeh told us what had happened while the prison burned. The zaptiehs suspected her and carried her into the burning building and left her.

It was almost dawn Saturday morning when Lusanne and I returned to mother. "As God wills, so be it," was all she said when we told her what had happened at the prison. She said there had been a great celebration in the El Hasan mosque, in honor of the Mohammedan Sunday, while we were at Gwazim. A special imam, or prayer reader, had come all the way from Trebizond to read special prayers set aside for such great events as the beginning of a holy war or massacre of Christians.

That morning soldiers went through the streets posting a new paper on the walls. It was what we had feared — an order from the Governor that all Armenian Christian women in the city, young and old, must be ready in three days to leave their homes and be deported — where, the order did not say.

As soon as the Turkish residents heard of the new order, many of them began to go about the Armenian half of the town offering to buy what the Armenian women wanted to sell. As there were none of the men left, the women had no one to advise them. To our house, which was one of the best in the city, there came many rich Turks, who told us we had better sell them our rugs and the beautiful laces mother, Lusanne and I had made.

Every Armenian girl is taught to make pretty laces. No girl is happy until she can make for herself a lace bridal veil. Always the Turks are eager to buy these, as they sell for much money to foreign traders, but no Armenian bride will sell her veil unless she is starving. Lusanne and I had made our veils, and had put them away until we should need them. We knew we could not carry them with us when we were deported, as they would soon be stolen. So we sold them, and mother's, too. The most we could get was a few piasters. Since I have come to America I have seen spreads and table covers, made from such bridal veils as ours, for sale in shops for hundreds of dollars. Father had brought us many rugs from Harpout, Smyrna and Damascus. For these mother could get only a few pennies.

On the second day after the proclamation, which was our Sunday, the soldiers visited all the houses. They walked in without knocking. They pretended to be looking for guns and revolvers, but what they took was our silver and gold spoons and vases.

That afternoon a company of horsemen rode past our house. We ran to the window and saw they were Aghja Daghi Kurds, the cruelest of all the tribes. At their head rode the famous Musa Bey, the chieftain who, a few years before, had waylaid Dr. Raynolds and Dr. Knapp, the famous American missionaries, and had robbed them and left them tied together on the road.

The Kurds rode to the palace of Husein Pasha. In a little while they rode away again, and some of the Pasha's soldiers rode with them. That meant, we knew, that the Governor had given the Kurds permission to waylay us when we were outside the city.

All that night the women sat up in their homes. In our house mother went from room to room, looking at the little things on the walls and in the cupboards that had been hers since she was a little girl. She sat a long time over father's clothes. I got out my playthings and cried over them. Some of them had been my grandmother's toys. Lusanne did not cry. She thought only of Andranik and the loss of her bridal veil, and her tears had dried, like mother's. Little Hovnan and Mardiros, our brothers, and Sarah and Aruciag, our sisters, cried very hard when we told they must say good-by to their dolls and their kites.

When morning of the last day came, I slipped out of our home to visit Mariam, my playmate, who lived a few doors away. Mariam's family was not very rich, and mother had said I might give her twenty liras from our money, that she might have it to bribe soldiers for protection. But Mariam was not there.

During the night zaptiehs had entered her house and taken her out of her bed, with just her nightdress on, and had carried her away. The soldiers said Rehim Bey had promised them money if they would bring Mariam to his house. Mariam's mother and little brother were kneeling beside her empty bed when I found them.

On my way back to our house a Turk stopped me. He asked me to go with him. He said I might as well, as "all the pretty Christian girls would have to give themselves to Turks or be killed anyway." I broke away and ran home as fast as I could. I could not forget the look on that Turk's face as he spoke to me. It was the first time I had ever seen such a look in a man's face. I tried to explain to mother. She put her arms around me, but all she said was:

"My poor little girl!"

The women had been allowed until noon to assemble in the square. Already they were arriving there, with horse, donkey and ox carts, some with as many of their things as they could heap on their carts, others with just blankets and comforts, a favorite rug and bread and fruits. In Armenia every family keeps a year's supply of food on hand. The women had to leave behind all they could not carry.

When it came time for us to go, I thought again of the look in that Turk's face. For the first time I realized just what it would mean to be a captive in one of the harems of the rich Turks whose big houses look down from the hills all about the city. I had heard of the Christian girls forced into haremliks of these houses, but I had never really understood. Lusanne was older. She knew more than I. "If only I could have died with Andranik," she said.

Mother thought of a plan she hoped might save Lusanne and me from the harems or a worse fate among the Kurds and soldiers. She brought out two yashmaks, or veils, such as Turkish women wear on the street, and made us put them on, hiding our faces. Over these she had us put on a feradjeh, a Turkish woman's cloak. We looked quite as if we were Turkish women, with all our faces hidden.

"It is only death that faces me, but for you, my daughters, there are even greater perils," mother said to us. "You will be able now to walk in the streets and the soldiers will think you are Mohammedan women. Try to reach Miss Graham, at the orphanage. Perhaps she can hide you until there is a way for you to escape into the north, where the sea is. And if you do find safety, thank God, and remember He is always with you." Then she kissed us and bade us go.

Miss Graham, who was an English girl, had come to our city from the American College at Marsovan, to teach in our school for orphaned Armenian girls. She was very young and pretty. The Turks had seemed to respect her, and mother thought we would be safe with her.

While mother went to the square with Aruciag, Sarah, Hovnan and Mardiros, Lusanne and I mingled with Mohammedan women who had gathered to watch the scenes at the square and to bargain for pieces of jewelry and other things the Armenian women knew they must either sell or have stolen from them. We planned to wait until dark before venturing to reach Miss Graham's.

Soon we saw Turks, both rich citizens and military officers, walking about in the square roughly examining the Christian girls. When they were pleased by a girl's appearance these beys and aghas tried to persuade their mothers to let them profess Mohammedanism and go away with them, promising to save her relatives from deportation. When mothers refused, the Turks often struck them. Officers killed some mothers who clung too closely to their daughters.

Many young girls gave in to the Turks and agreed to swear faith in Allah for the sake of their mothers, sisters and brothers. Toward evening the khateeb, or keeper of the mosque, was brought to receive their "conversions."

More than fifty girls took the oath. Just as soon as the oaths were all taken the officers signaled to the zaptiehs and they took all these girls away from their families and gathered them at one side of the square. Then the richer beys began to examine the apostatized girls. The soldiers would give a girl to the one who paid them the most money, unless an officer also wanted her. The higher military officers were given first choice.

One by one the soldiers dragged the girls who had sacrificed their religion in vain to save their mothers and relatives out of the square and toward the homes of the Turks. Lusanne and I had gone close to watch our chance to speak once more to mother. We saw everything. And while they were taking the girls away, we saw a zaptieh carrying Miss Graham in his arms. She struggled hard, but the zaptieh was too strong. We learned afterward the soldiers had gone to her school to get the little Armenian girls, and when Miss Graham tried to fight them, they said her country couldn't help her now, and since she was a Christian they would take her, too.

It was to Rehim Bey's house, where Mariam already had been carried, they took Miss Graham. They did not even try to make her become a Mohammedan. Rehim Bey was very powerful, and was a cousin of Talaat Bey, the Minister of the Interior at Constantinople.

III

VAHBY BEY TAKES HIS CHOICE

FOR a time Lusanne and I debated whether we should return to the square and join mother, since Miss Graham had been stolen and could not help us, or whether we should make an effort to escape since we had so far escaped notice in our disguises. We decided that, perhaps, if we could reach the house of a friendly Turk, outside the city, and we knew of many of these, we might find a way to help mother. We did not know how this could ever be done, but we clung to a hope that surely someone would aid us.

When it was quite dark, we crept through side streets to our deserted house and succeeded in getting into the garden without attracting attention. We dared not make a light, or remain on the lower floors, soldiers might enter the house at any moment. The safest place to hide, we thought, would be the attic.

In the attic there were a number of boxes of old things of mother's. We searched until we found some old clothes, and each of us put on an old dress of mother's under the cloaks she had given us. If we were discovered, the old clothes, we thought, might deceive the Turks if we could keep our faces covered. Neither Lusanne nor I had slept during the three days the Turks allowed the Armenian women to prepare for deportation. Toward morning we were both so worn out we fell asleep. Suddenly I awoke to find an ugly zaptieh standing over me, a sword in his hand. He had kicked me. Three or four others, who, with the leader, had broken in to search for valuables, were coming up the ladder into the attic, and the one who had found us was calling out to them:

"Mouhadjirler — anleri keselim!" — ("Here are refugees — let's kill them!")

The zaptieh's shout awakened Lusanne and she screamed.

By this time the Turks had pulled me to my feet, but when Lusanne screamed they dropped me. "That's no old one," the chief zaptieh said, as he turned to my sister. "Her voice is young."

They kicked me aside while they gathered around Lusanne, picked her up and carried her down the ladder to the floor below, where our bedrooms were. There they found a lamp and lighted it from the torch one of them carried. They began to examine Lusanne, who screamed and fought them desperately. I followed them down the ladder and ran into the room, but when they saw me one of them struck me with his fists, and I fell. They thought I at least was as old as my clothes looked. One of them said, "Stick the old one on a bayonet if she don't keep still." I could do nothing but stay on the floor, crouch tight to the wall and look on.

A zaptieh tore off Lusanne's veil and cloak. When they saw her face and that she was young and good looking, they shouted and laughed. The leader dropped his gun and laid his sword on a table and then took Lusanne away from the others and held her in his arms. She fought so hard the others had to help hold her while the officer kissed her. Each time he kissed her he laughed and all the others laughed too. One by one, the zaptiehs caressed her, each passing her to the other, all much amused by her struggles.

When Lusanne's dress was all torn and her screams grew weak, I could not stand it any longer. I crept up to the men on my knees and begged them to stop. I knew there was no longer any hope that we might escape, so I pleaded: "Please take us to the square to our relatives; we will get money for you if you will only spare us."

They allowed us to leave the house, but followed across the street to the square. It was daylight now and the women were stirring about, sharing with each other the bread and meats some had brought with them. The zaptiehs made Lusanne stay with them while I searched for mother. She was caring for a baby whose mother had died during the night. The first thing she asked was, "Where is Lusanne — have they got her?"

42

Mother gave me two liras. The zaptiehs took them and shoved Lusanne away. She fainted when she realized they had released her. During the first day and night no one knew what was to happen. Such of the soldiers as would answer questions said only that the Pasha had ordered the women deported. None knew how or when. During the first night three of the mothers of girls who had been taken by the Turks the day before died. One of them killed herself while her other children were sleeping around her. So many were crowded into the square not all could find room to lie down and the soldiers killed any who attempted to move into the street.

In the center of the square, there was a band-stand, where the Mutassarif's band often played in the summer evenings. In this band-stand the soldiers had put the little girls and boys taken from the Christian Orphanage when they carried off Miss Graham. There were thirty little girls, none of them more than twelve years old, and almost as many boys.

The children were crying bitterly when Lusanne and I, at mother's suggestion, went to see if we could not help care for them. There was no food for them except what the women could spare from their own stores. The Turks never give food to their prisoners. Toward noon of that day Vahby Bey, the military commandant of the whole vilayet, who had under him almost an army corps, rode into the city with his staff and a company of hamidieh, or Kurdish cavalry. He was on his way to Harpout, from Erzindjan, a big city in the north, where he had attended a council of war with Enver Pasha, the Turkish Commander-in-Chief.

Vahby Bey walked from his headquarters into the public square, accompanied by his staff. Hundreds of women crowded around him, but his staff officers beat them away with swords and canes. The general walked at once to the band-stand and looked at the children. Abdoullah Bey, the chief of the gendarmes, was with him, and they talked in low voices.

When Vahby Bey had gone, several officers began to ask Armenian girls if they would like to accompany the orphans and take care of them in the place where the government would put them. The officers said they would take several girls for this purpose, and thus save them the terrors of deportation and death, or worse, if they would first agree to become Mohammedan.

Many mothers thought this was the only way to save their daughters from the harem. Some of the younger women, among them brides whose husbands had been killed, were so discouraged and frightened they were eager to accept this chance. The officers said only young girls would be accepted, and bade all who wanted to take advantage of the opportunity to gather at the band-stand. More than two hundred assembled, with mothers and relatives hanging onto them. I don't think any of them really was willing to forswear Christ, but they thought they would be forgiven if they seemed to do so to save themselves from being massacred, stolen in the desert or forced to be concubines.

A hamidieh officer, looking smart and neat in his costly uniform, went to the stand to select the girls. He chose twelve of the very prettiest. One girl who was tall and very handsome, and whose father had been a rich merchant, refused to take the Mohammedan oath unless her two sisters, both younger, also were accepted. The officer consented. The three girls had no mother, only some younger brothers, and these the officers said might accompany the orphans. The three sisters were very glad they were to be saved. One of them was a friend of Lusanne's, and to her she said: "Our God will know why we are doing this; we will always pray to Him in secret." Esther Magurditch, daughter of Boghos Artin, a great Armenian author and poet, who lived in our city, also was willing to take the oath, and was chosen. Esther had been one of my playmates. Her mother was an English woman, who had married her father when he was traveling in Europe. Esther had married Vartan Magurditch, a young lawyer, just a week before. When both her father and husband were taken from her, she almost lost her mind.

When all the fourteen girls had said the Mohammedan rek'ah, soldiers took them with the orphans to the big house in which Esther's family had lived. It was the largest Armenian home in the city.

As soon as the children and the apostatized girls entered the house, Esther prepared a meal for them from the bread and other

44

food that had been left. While the children were eating, the girls were summoned to another part of the house, where an aged Mohammedan woman awaited them with yashmaks, or Turkish veils, which she told them they must put on, as they had become Mohammedan women and must not let their faces be seen.

The young women were then told to seat themselves until an officer came to give further instructions. They still were waiting in the room when childish voices in the other part of the house were lifted up, in screams. The girls rushed to the door, only to find it locked.

Suddenly the door opened and Vahby Bey, with his chief of staff, Ferid Bey, and Ali Riza Effendi, the Police Commissary, whose headquarters were in Harpout, entered. With them were a number of other smartly dressed officers, who had been traveling with General Vahby. The girls fell to their knees before the officers, and asked them, in Allah's name, to let them go to the children. The officers laughed. The three sisters, who had taken their little brothers with the other children, appealed to General Vahby to tell them what had happened to their little ones. Vahby Bey did not answer, but pointed to the taller one of the three girls, the one who was so handsome, and said to the chief of staff: "This one I will take; guard her carefully." Ferid Bey, the chief officer, then called some soldiers, who picked up the girl and carried her upstairs to a room which Vahby Bey had occupied. Vahby Bey followed. Ferid Bey then selected Esther, and soldiers carried her up to another room. Ferid Bey followed and dismissed the soldiers, with orders to place a guard outside his door and another outside the door of Vahby Bey's room.

Downstairs the other officers of Vahby Bey's staff each selected a girl, the officers of higher rank taking first choice. There were three girls left, one of them the youngest sister of the girl Vahby Bey had taken, and the soldiers took possession of these, not even removing them from the room.

How long these three girls lived I cannot tell. It was Esther who told us what happened that afternoon in her house, for she was the only one of the fourteen who escaped alive. Before she got

45

away from the house she looked into the room where the soldiers had been, and saw that the three girls were dead.

Esther tried to resist Ferid Bey, and to plead with him; but he threatened to kill her. When she told him she would rather die, he opened the door so she could see the men standing guard in the hall, and said to her:

"Very well then; if you do not be quiet, I will give you to the soldiers!"

Surely God will not blame Esther for shrinking away from the sight of those many men and allowing Ferid Bey, who was only one man, to remain.

The officers busied themselves with the girls until evening. When Ferid Bey left her, Esther begged him again to at least tell her where the children were, that she might go to them. He had assured her during the afternoon that the orphans were safe, and that the girls could return to them later. Now he pretended no longer. "We have no time to bother with the children of unbelievers," he said. "We drowned them in the river!"

Ferid Bey told the truth. We found some of their bodies when we passed that way later on. The soldiers had tied the children together with ropes in groups of ten and had driven them to Kara Su, also a branch of the Euphrates, ten miles away. Those who were too little to walk or keep up with the others, the soldiers had killed with their bayonets or gun handles. They left their bodies, still tied together, at the roadside. On the river banks we found other bodies that had been washed up.

As soon as Ferid Bey had gone and Esther heard the other officers assembling on the floor below, something warned her to try to escape immediately. Her clothes had been nearly all torn away, but she dared not wait even to cover herself. She climbed onto the roof by a small stairway which the Turks were not guarding, and hid herself there.

General Vahby and his officers went to their quarters. The soldiers hunted out the girls they had left behind. Esther heard them fighting among themselves over the prettiest ones. After a time, most of the girls died. The soldiers killed the rest with their swords when they were finished with, them. From what Esther heard them saying to each other as they did this, she believed they had been ordered not to leave any of the young women alive as witnesses to Vahby Bey and his officers having done such things openly.

Esther crept out of the house and crawled through a back street to the square. She found my mother and fell into her arms. When daylight came a soldier saw her and recognized her as one of the girls who had apostatized the day before, and the zaptiehs carried her away. At noon more soldiers came to the square, with zaptiehs and hamidieh, and officers began to go among us, saying that within one hour we were to march. They told us we were to be taken to Harpout, but we soon saw our destination was in the direction of Arabkir.

That last hour in our city, which had been the home of many of our family ancestors for centuries, and beyond the borders of which but few of our neighbors ever had traveled, was spent by most of the mothers and their children in prayer. There was almost no more weeping or wailing. The strong, young women gathered close to them the aged ones or frail mothers with very young babies. Each of us who had more strength than for our own needs tried to find someone who needed a share of it.

We were encouraged a little when the time came for us to move by the apparent kindness of some of the new Turkish soldiers, who seemed to want to make us as comfortable as possible. It was at the suggestion of these that many aged grandmothers whose daughters had more than one baby were placed together in a group of ox carts, each with a grandchild that had been weaned. The soldiers said this plan would relieve the young mothers of so many children to watch over, and would let the old women have company, while, being together, the soldiers could keep them comfortable.

When we were three hours out from town these ox carts fell behind. Presently the soldiers that had been detailed to stay with them joined the rest of the party ahead. When we asked where the grandmothers and the babies were, the soldiers replied: "They were too much trouble. We killed them!"

It was very hot, and the roads were dusty, with no shade. Many women and children soon fell to the ground exhausted. The zaptiehs beat these with their clubs. Those who couldn't get up and walk as fast as the rest were beaten till they died, or they were killed outright.

Our first intimation of what might happen to us at any time came when we had been on the road four hours. We came then to a little spot where there were trees and a spring. The soldiers who marched afoot were themselves tired, and gave us permission to rest a while, and get water.

A woman pointed onto the plain where, a little way from the road, we saw what seemed to be a human being, sitting on the ground. Some of us walked that way and saw it was an Armenian woman. On the ground beside her were six bundles of different sizes, from a very little one to one as large as I would be, each wrapped in spotless white that glistened in the sun.

We did not need to ask to know that in each of the bundles was the body of a child. The mother's face was partially covered with a veil, which told us she had given up God in the hope of saving her little ones — but in vain!

She did not speak or move, only looked at us with a great sadness in her eyes. Her face seemed familiar and one of us knelt beside her and gently lifted her veil. Then we recognized her — Margarid, wife of the pastor, Badvelli Moses, of Kamakh, a little city thirty miles to the north. Badvelli Moses once had been a teacher in our school at Tchemesh-Gedzak. He was a graduate of the college at Harpout, and Margarid had graduated from a Seminary at Mezre. They were much beloved by all who knew them. Often Badvelli Moses had returned, with his wife and Sherin, their oldest daughter, who was my age, to Tchemesh-Gedzak to visit and speak in our churches. Besides Sherin, there were five smaller girls and boys. All were there, by Margarid's side, wrapped in the sheets she had carried with her when the people of her city were deported.

"There were a thousand of us," Margarid said when we had brought her out of the stupor of grief which had overcome her. "They took us away with only an hour's notice. The first night,

Kurdish bandits rode down upon us and took all the men a little way off and killed them. We saw our husbands die, one by one. They stripped all the women and children — even the littlest ones — so they could search our bodies for money. They took all the pretty girls and violated them before our eyes.

"I pleaded with the commander of our soldier guards to protect my Sherin. He had been our friend in Kamakh. He promised to save us if I would become a Moslem, and for Sherin's sake, I did. He made the bandits allow us to put on our clothes again, and Sherin and I veiled our faces.

"The commander detailed soldiers to escort us to Harpout and take me to the governor there. When we left, the Kurds and soldiers who were tired of the girls were killing them, and the others as well. When we reached here, the soldiers killed my little ones by mashing their heads together. They violated Sherin while they held me, and then cut off her breasts, so that she died. They left me alive, they said, because I had become Moslem."

We tried to take Margarid into our party, but she would not come. "I must go to God with my children," she said. "I will stay here until He takes me." So we left her sitting there with her loved ones.

It was late at night and the stars were out when we arrived at the banks of the Kara Su. Here we were told by the soldiers we could camp for the night. In the distance, we could see the light on the minaret in the village of Gwazim, where father and Paul had died in the burning prison.

All along the road, zaptiehs killed women and children who could not keep up with the party, and many of the pretty girls had been dragged to the side of the road, to be sent back to the party later with tears and shame in their faces. Lusanne and I had daubed our faces with mud to make us ugly, and I still wore my cloak and veil.

For a time it seemed as if we were not to be molested, as the guards remained in little groups, away from us. Only the scream now and then of a girl who had attracted some soldier's attention reminded us we must not sleep.

IV

THE CRUEL SMILE OF KEMAL EFFENDI

DURING the night, Turkish residents from cities nearby came to our camp and sought to buy whatever the women had brought with them of value. Many had brought a piece of treasured lace; others had carried their jewelry; some even had brought articles of silver, and rugs. There were many horse and donkey carts along, as the Turks encouraged all the women to carry as much of their belongings as they could. This we soon learned was done to swell the booty for the soldiers when the party was completely at their mercy.

As the civilian Turks went through the camp that night, they bargained also for girls and young women. One of them urged mother to let him take Lusanne. When mother refused, he said to her:

"You might as well let me have her. I will treat her kindly and she can work with my other servants. She will be sold or stolen anyway, if she is not killed. None of you will live very long." Several children were stolen early in the night by these Turks. One little girl of nine years was picked up a few feet away from me and carried screaming away. When her relatives complained to the soldiers, they were told to be glad she had escaped the long walk to the Syrian desert, where the rest of the party was to be taken.

Dawn was just breaking, and we were thankful that the sleepless, horrible first night was so nearly over, when, in a great cloud of sand and dust, the Aghja Daghi Kurds, with Musa Bey at their head, rode down upon us. The soldiers must have known they were coming, for they had gathered quite a way from the camp, and were not surprised. Perhaps it was arranged when Musa Bey visited Husein Pasha, in Tchemesh-Gedzak, just before we were taken away.

The horses of the Kurds galloped down all who were in their way, their hoofs sinking into the heads and bodies of scores of frightened women. The riders quickly gathered up all the donkeys and horses belonging to the families, and when these had been driven off, they dismounted and began to walk among us and pick out young women to steal. Lusanne and I clung close to mother, who tried to hide us, but one of three Kurds who walked near us saw me.

He stopped and tore my veil away. When he saw the mud and dirt on my face, he roughly rubbed it off with his hands, jerking me to my feet, to look closer. When he saw I really was young, despite my disguise, he shouted. One of the other Kurds turned quickly and came up. When I looked up into his face, I saw it was Musa Bey himself!

The bey clutched at me roughly, tore open my dress and threw back my hair. Then he gave a short command, and, so quickly, I had hardly screamed, he threw me across his horse and leaped up behind. In another instant he was carrying me in a wild gallop across the plains. His band rode close behind, each Kurd holding a girl across his horse. I struggled with all my strength to get free. I wanted to throw myself under the horse's hoofs and be trampled to death. But the bey held me across his horse's shoulder with a grip of iron, as he galloped to the west, skirting the banks of the river.

I screamed for my mother. The other girls' screams joined with mine. Behind us I could hear the shouts and cries of our party. I thought I heard my mother's voice among them. Then the shouts died away in the distance. Soon I lost consciousness.

When I came to, I was lying on the ground, with the other girls who had been stolen. The Kurds had dismounted. Some were busy making camp, while others were in groups amusing themselves with such of the girls as were not exhausted. Musa Bey was absent.

My clothes were torn and my body ached from the jolting of the horse. My shoes and stockings were off when the Kurds came down upon us, so my feet were bare. For a long time I lay quietly, fearing to move lest I attract attention and suffer as some of the girls already were suffering. When I could look around, I saw that among the girls were several whom I had known, and some I recognized as young married women. Some I knew were mothers who had left babies behind.

On the ground near me was quite a little girl, Maritza, whose mother had been killed by the zaptiehs just after we left Tchemesh-Gedzak. She had carried a baby brother in her arms during all the long walk of the first day on the road. She was weeping silently. I crawled over to her.

"When they picked me up, I was holding little Marcar," she sobbed. "The Kurds tore him out of my arms and threw him out on the ground. It killed him. I can't see anything else but his little body when it fell."

It was several hours before Musa Bey came back. A party of Turks on horseback rode up with him. They came from the West where there were many little villages along the river banks, some of them the homes of rich Moslems.

When they dismounted, Musa Bey began to exhibit the girls he had stolen to the Turks. Some of the Turks, I could tell, were wealthy farmers. Others seemed to be rich beys or aghas (influential citizens). Musa Bey made us all stand up. Those who didn't obey him quick enough he struck with his whip. When I got up off the ground, he caught me by the shoulder and threw me down again. "You lie still," he said. I saw that he did the same thing to two or three other girls.

The Turks brutally examined the girls Musa Bey showed them, and began to pick them out. Those who were farmers chose the older ones, who seemed stronger than the rest. The others wanted the prettiest of the girls, and argued among themselves over a choice.

The farmers wanted the girls to work as slaves in the field. The others wanted girls for a different purpose — for their harems or as household slaves, or for the concubine markets of Smyrna and Constantinople. Musa Bey demanded ten medjidiehs, or about eight dollars, American money, apiece. I thought, as I lay trembling on the ground, what a little bit of money that was for a Christian soul.

Little Maritza, who stood close to me, was taken by a Turk who seemed to be very old. Another man wanted her, but the old one offered Musa Bey four medjidiehs more, and the other turned away to pick out another girl. The Turk who bought Maritza was afraid to take her away on his horse, so he bargained with Musa Bey until he had promised two extra medjidiehs if a Kurd would carry her to his house. Musa Bey gave an order and a Kurd climbed onto his horse, lifted Maritza in front of him and rode away by the side of the man who had bought her. She did not cry any more, but just held her hands in front of her eyes.

After a while, all the girls were gone but me and the few others whom Musa Bey had not offered for sale. The ones who were bought by the farmers were destined to work in the fields, and they were the most fortunate, for sometimes the Turkish farmer is kind and gentle. Those who were bought for the harem faced the untold heartache of the girl to whom some things are worse than death.

When the last of the Turks had gone with their human property, Musa Bey spoke to his followers and some of them came toward us. We thought we had been reserved for Musa Bey himself, and we began to scream and plead. They picked us up despite our cries and mounted horses with us. Musa Bey leaped onto his horse and we were again carried away, with Musa Bey leading.

I begged the Kurd who carried me to tell me where we were going. He would not answer. We had ridden for two hours, until late in the afternoon, when we came to the outskirts of a village. We rode into the yard of a large stone house surrounded by a crumbling stone wall. It was a very ancient house, and before we had stopped in the courtyard I recognized it from a description in our school books, as a castle which had been built by the Saracens, and restored a hundred years ago by a rich Turk, who was a favorite of the Sultan who then reigned.

I remembered, as the Kurds lifted us down from their horses, that the castle was now the home of Kemal Effendi, a member of the Committee of Union and Progress, the powerful organization of the Young Turks. He was reputed throughout our district as being

53

very bitter toward Christians, and there were many stories told in our country of Christian girls who had been stolen from their homes and taken to him, never to be heard from again.

Only a part of the castle had been repaired so it might be lived in, and it was toward this part of the building the Kurds took us when they had dismounted. I tried to plead with the Kurd who had me, but he shook me roughly. We were led into a small room. There were servants, both men and women, in this room, and they began to talk about us and examine us. Musa Bey drove them to tell their master he had arrived.

In a little while Kemal Effendi entered. He was very tall and middle aged. His eyes made me tremble when they looked at me. I could only shudder as I remembered the things that were said of him.

When Kemal Effendi had looked at all of us for minutes that seemed torturing hours, he seemed satisfied. He spoke to Musa Bey and the Kurds went out, followed by him. I do not know how much Musa Bey was paid for us.

Women came into the room and tried to be kind to us. One of them put her arms around me and asked me to not weep. She told me I was very fortunate in falling into such good hands as Kemal Effendi. "He will be gentle to you. You must obey him and be affectionate and he will treat you as he does his wife. He will not be cruel unless you are disobedient," the woman said. I do not know what was her position in the house, but I think she was a servant who had been a concubine when she was younger.

Until then, I had tried to keep myself from thinking that I had lost my mother and sisters and brothers. What the woman told us was to happen to us in the house of Kemal took away my hopes of ever seeing them again. I told her I would kill myself if I could not go back to my relatives.

It was late in the evening before Kemal Effendi summoned us. He had eaten and seemed to be gracious. One of the girls, who had been a bride, threw herself on the floor before him, weeping and begging him to set us free. Kemal Effendi lost his good humor at once. He called a man servant and told him to take the girl away. "Shut her up till she learns when to weep and when to laugh," he

54

ordered. The man carried the girl out screaming. Kemal then asked us about our families, how old we were, and if we would renounce our religion and say the Mohammedan oath. One girl, whose name I do not know, but whom I had often seen in our Sunday school at Tchemesh-Gedzak was not brave enough to refuse. The Kurds had treated her cruelly, and the one who had carried her away had beaten her when she cried. She moaned, "Yes, yes, God has deserted me. I will be true to Mohammed. Please don't beat me any more."

When she had said this, Kemal smiled and put his hand on her head. "You are wise. You will not be punished if you continue so."

The second girl would not forsake Christ. "You may kill me if you wish," she said, "and then I will go to Jesus Christ." As soon as she had said this, a man servant dragged her out of the room. I looked at Kemal Effendi, but he was still smiling, as soft and smoothly as if he could not be otherwise than very gentle. I could see that he was more cruel even than people had said of him.

When Kemal Effendi spoke to me, his voice was very soft. I can still remember it made me feel as if some wild animal's tongue was caressing my face.

"And you, my girl," he said, "are you to be wise or foolish?"

"God save me," I whispered to myself again, and then something seemed to whisper back. I heard myself saying, without thinking of the words, "I will try to be as you wish."

"That is very good. You will be happy," Kemal replied. "You will acknowledge Allah as God and Mohammed as his prophet? Then I will be kind to you."

"I will do that, Effendi, and I will be obedient, if you will save my family also," I said.

"And if I do not?" Kemal asked.

"Then I will die," I replied.

The Effendi looked at me a long time. Then he asked me to tell him of my family. I told him of my mother, my sister, Lusanne, and of my other sisters and brothers. He made me stand close to him. He put his hands on me. I stood very straight and looked into his face. I promised that if he would take my mother and sisters and brothers also, I would not only renounce my religion, but obey him in all things. And for each thing I promised, I whispered to myself, "Please, God, forgive me." But I could think of no other way. I was afraid that even now, perhaps, my mother, brothers and sisters were being murdered. It seemed as if my body and soul were such little things to give for them.

Kemal kept me with him more than an hour, I think. Each time he tried to touch me, I shrank away from him. It amused him, for he would laugh and clap his hands, as if very pleased. "I will die first," I said each time, "unless you save my family."

I had begun to lose hope; to think Kemal was but playing with me. I could hardly keep my tears back, yet I did not want to weep for I knew he would be displeased. Then, suddenly, he appeared to have made up his mind. He arose and looked down at me.

"Very well. The bargain is made. I will protect your relatives. I prefer a willing woman to a sulky one. We will go to-morrow and bring them."

I would have been happy, even in my sacrifice, had it not been that Kemal Effendi smiled as he said this — that cruel, wicked smile. I would have believed in him if he had not smiled. But I felt as plain as if it were spoken to me that behind that smile was some wicked thought.

I begged him to go with me then to bring my people before it was too late. He said it would not be too late in the morning; that he would go with me after sunrise; that I need have no further fears. When he left the room, the woman who had spoken to me earlier came in to me. She took me into the haremlik, or women's quarters, where there were many other women.

I think the harem women would have been sorry for me had they dared. They tried to cheer me. They asked much about our religion, and why Armenians would die rather than adopt the religion of the Turks. I could not talk to them, because I could think only of the morning — whether I would be in time — and wonder what could be behind that smile of the Effendi's.

They put me in a small room, hardly as large as an American closet. They told me an Imam would come the next day to take my oath.

They did not know the Effendi had promised to save my relatives and bring them to the house.

I had not been alone in my room very long when a pretty odalik, a young slave girl, slipped silently through the curtained door and took my hand in hers. She was a Syrian, she told me, whose father had sold her when she was very young. She had been sent from Smyrna to the house of Kemal. She was the favorite slave of the Effendi. She wanted to tell me that if I needed someone to confide in when her master had made me his slave, too, I could trust her. She said she was supposed to have become Mohammedan, but that secretly she was still Christian. She did not know many prayers she explained, for she was so young when her father had been compelled to sell her. She wanted me to teach her new ones.

It was so comforting to have someone to whom I could talk through the long hours of waiting until sunrise. I told the little odalik I had promised to be a Moslem only to save my mother and sisters and brothers. I told her what Kemal had promised, how he had smiled and how I feared something I could not explain.

"When he smiles, he does not mean what he says," the girl said, sadly. "Often when he is displeased with me, he smiles and pets me. Soon afterwards I am whipped. When the Kurd, Musa Bey, who brought you, came to tell the Effendi he had stolen some girls and wished to sell the prettiest to him, the Effendi smiled and said, 'Be good to the best appearing ones, and bring them here.' I would not trust him to keep his promise."

Early in the morning the Effendi sent for me and asked me to describe my relatives. I told him it would be impossible for him to find them in so large a party. He agreed I should go with him and we set out, he riding his horse while I walked beside him. I tried to convince him I was contented with the bargain we had made — even that I was glad of the opportunity to have his protection. Yet I knew that behind his smile was his resolve to have my family killed as soon as he had brought about my "conversion" and had obtained the willing sacrifice he desired.

Kemal knew the party in which my family was would be taken across the river at the fording place to the north. We went in that direction, but they had not yet arrived and we turned back to meet them.

When we came close to the river bank, which was high and cliff-like, I looked down at the water and saw it was running red with blood, with here and there a body floating on the surface. I screamed when I saw this, and sank to the ground. I shut my eyes, yet I seemed to see what had happened — a company of Armenians taken to the river bank and massacred, cut with knives and sabres before they were thrown into the river, else they would not have stained the river for many miles.

The Effendi reproached me.

"Christians are learning their God cannot save their blood. It is what they deserve. Why should you weep now, my little one, when already you have decided to give your faith to Islam?" I could not look at him, but somehow I could feel that in his eyes there would be the gleam of that terrible smile.

I gathered strength and replied firmly: "I am not used to blood, Effendi."

We went on, close by the river, looking for the vanguard of my people who would come from the south. The river banks reached higher, and the river narrowed until it was almost a solid red with the blood. Afterwards I learned seven hundred men and boys from Erzindjan had been convoyed to the river and killed by zaptiehs. The zaptiehs stabbed them one by one and then threw them into the river. And this river was a part of the Euphrates of the Bible, with its source in the Garden of Eden! Kemal rode dose to the high banks. I walked at his side. Below me the river seemed to call me to security. If I went on, I knew Kemal would only feed false hopes by promising protection to my relatives he would soon tire of giving. And I would have to make the sacrifice he demanded in vain. I waited until we were at the very edge of the cliff. Then I jumped.

I heard the curse of Kemal Effendi as I struck the red water. When I came to the surface, I saw him sitting on his horse at the top of the cliff, looking down at me. I was glad I could not tell if he were smiling.

I had learned to swim when I was very young. Unconsciously I struck out for the opposite shore and reached it safely. The banks were not so high on that side. Soon I was free. It must have been that Kemal did not have a revolver or he would have shot me. I did not look back, but ran onto the plain. I did not know if Kemal would send searchers for me, so I hid in the sand, covering myself so Kurds or zaptiehs could not see me if they rode near, until I saw the long line of my people from Tchemesh-Gedzak approaching on the other side of the river.

I remained through the rest of the day and night, while the refugees camped at the fording place. When they crossed the river the next morning, I managed to get in among them during the confusion. My mother was so happy she could not speak for a long time. Kemal Effendi had ridden up to them, she told me, and had demanded that the leader of the zaptiehs find my relatives and punish them for my escape. Mother bribed the soldiers and they told Kemal my relatives were not among the party.

The party was given no opportunity to rest after the laborious fording of the river, but was made to push on toward Arabkir. Little Hovnan and Mardiros, and Aruciag and Sarah, already were almost exhausted. Their little feet were torn and bleeding, and mother and Lusanne kept them wrapped in cloths. There were no more babies in the party, for just before they forded the river the zaptiehs made the mothers of the youngest babies leave them behind. The mothers nursed them while they were waiting to be taken over the river and then laid them in little rows on the river bank and left them.

The soldiers said Mohammedan women would come out from a nearby village to take the babies and care for them, but none came while we still could see the spot where they were left, and that was for several hours. Several of the mothers, when they realized the promise of the soldiers was just a ruse, jumped into the river to swim back. The soldiers shot them in the water. After that we were not allowed to go near the river, even to drink.

Late that day we came to a khan, or travelers' rest house, such as are found along all the roads in Asia Minor, maintained after an ancient custom of the Turks as stopping places for caravans. We were told we could rest there for the remainder of the day and night, but when we drew near the khan, a party of soldiers came out and halted us. We could not go to the building, our guards were told, as it was occupied by travelers being taken north to Shabin Kara-Hissar, a large city in the district of Trebizond near the Black Sea.

Soon we learned who these travelers were. They were a company of "turned" Armenians, as the Turks call Christians who have given up their religion. The company was from Keban-Maden, a city thirty miles south. The company arrived at the khan that morning, having traveled twenty miles the day before.

The zaptiehs who guarded our party and the soldiers who had come from Keban-Maden with the others, soon became friends and talked earnestly with each other. They had forbidden us to go near the khan, and we wondered why the "turned" Christians were not to be seen. Presently a slim young girl crept out of the house and, unseen by the soldiers, crawled along the ground until she came to the outskirts of our camp. She was naked and her feet were cut and bruised.

She was a bride, she said, who had "turned" with her young husband. The Mutassarif of Keban-Maden had promised all the Armenians in his city that their lives would be saved if they accepted Islam, the child-bride said, and more than four hundred of them, mostly the younger married people, agreed.

Then they were told, she said, they would have to go to Shabin Kara-Hissar. As soon as they were outside the city, the soldiers robbed them of everything worth taking. Then most of the soldiers returned to Keban-Maden so as not to miss the looting there of the Armenian houses. The soldiers that remained tied the men in groups of five and made them march bound in this way. During their first night on the road, the bride said, the soldiers stripped all the women of their clothing and made them march after that naked.

Terrible things happened during that night, the girl said. Nearly all the women were outraged, and when husbands who were still tied together, and were helpless to interfere while they looked on, cried out about it, the soldiers killed them. The little bride had come over to us to ask if some of us would not give her a piece of clothing to cover her body. Many of our women offered her underskirts and other garments, and she crawled back to the khan with as many as she could carry, for herself and other women.

They did not know what was going to happen to them. They did not believe the soldiers who said they would be permitted to live at Shabin Kara-Hissar in peace. Their guards already were grumbling, she said, at having to take such a long march with them just because they had "turned."

That night a dozen or more of our youngest girls, from eight to ten years old, were stolen by the soldiers and taken to the khan. We didn't know what became of them, but we feared they were taken to be sold to Mohammedan families, or to rich Turks. Mother slept that night, she was so worn out, but Lusanne and I took turns keeping guard over our sisters and brothers, keeping them covered with dirt and bits of clothing, so the soldiers as they prowled among us, would not see them.

Before daylight, the Armenians in the khan were taken away. We had not been upon the road next day but a few hours when we came upon a long row of bodies along the roadside, we recognized them as the men of the party of "turned" Armenians. A little farther on, we came to a well, but we found it choked with the naked corpses of the rest of the party — the women. The zaptiehs had killed all the party, and to prevent Armenians deported along that road later, from using the water, had thrown the bodies of the women into it.

V

THE WAYS OF THE ZAPTIEHS

While we stood, in groups, looking with horror into the well, I suddenly heard these words, spoken by a woman standing near me: "God has gone mad; we are deserted!"

I turned and saw it was the wife of Badvelli Markar, a pastor who had been our neighbor in Tchemesh-Gedzak. When the men of our city were massacred, the Badvelli's wife was left to care for an aged mother, who was then ill in bed with typhoid fever, and three children — a baby, a little girl of three, and a boy who was five. She had begged the Turks to let her remain in her home to care for her mother, but they refused. They made the aged woman leave her bed and take to the road with the rest of us. She died the first day.

During the first days, we were on the road the Badvelli's wife was very courageous. Then her little boy died. The guards had compelled her to leave her baby at the river crossing and now her little girl, the last of her children, was ill in her arms. When we passed the bodies of the Armenians from the khan, laid along the road, the Badvelli's wife suddenly lost her mind.

"God has gone mad, I tell you — mad — mad — mad!"

This time, she shrieked it aloud and ran in among the others in our company, crying the terrible thing as she went. A woman tried to stop her, to take the little girl out of her arms, but she fought fiercely and held on to the child.

I have heard how sometimes a sickness like the plague will spread from one person to another with fatal quickness. That was how the madness of the Badvelli's wife spread through our party. It seemed hardly more than a minute before the awful cry was taken up by scores, even hundreds, of women whose minds already were shaken by their inability to understand why they should be made to suffer the things they had to endure at the hands of the Turks.

It was the mothers of young children, mostly, who gave in to the madness. Some of these threw their children on the ground and ran, screaming, out of the line and into the desert. Others ran wild with their children hanging to their arms. Their relatives tried to subdue them, but were powerless.

I think there were more than 200 women whose minds gave way under this sudden impulse, stirred by the crazed widow of the pastor.

The zaptiehs who were in charge of us could not understand at first. They thought there was a revolt. They charged in among us, swinging their swords and guns right and left, even shooting point blank. Many were killed or wounded hopelessly before the zaptiehs understood. Then the guards were greatly amused, and laughed. "See," they said; "that is what your God is — He is crazy." We could only bow our heads and submit to the taunt. Some of the women recovered their senses and were very sorry. Those who remained crazed the zaptiehs turned onto the plains to starve to death. They would not kill an insane person, as it is against their religion.

We had been told we were to go to Arabkir, but soon after leaving the khan we changed our direction. It was apparent we were headed in the direction of Hassan-Chelebi, a small city south of Arabkir. None of our guards would give us any definite information.

The zaptiehs made us march in a narrow line, but one or two families abreast. The line of weary stragglers stretched out as far as I could see, both ahead and behind. We had but little water, as the zaptiehs would not allow us to go near springs or streams, but compelled us to purchase water from the farmer Kurds who came out from villages along the way. The villagers demanded sometimes a lira (nearly $5.) a cup for water, and always the boys we sent out to buy it were sure to receive a beating as well as the water. We who had money with us had to share with those who

63

had none. Sometimes the villagers would sell the water, collect the money, and then tip over the cups.

After we were on the road a week, we were treated even more cruelly than during the first few days. The old women, and those who were too ill to keep on, were killed, one by one. The soldiers said they could not bother with them. When children lagged behind, or got out of the line to rest, the zaptiehs would lift them on their bayonets and toss them away — sometimes trying to catch them again as they fell, on their bayonet points. Mothers who saw their young ones killed in this way for the sport of our guards could not protest. We had learned that any sort of a protest was suicide. They had to watch and wring their hands, or hold their eyes shut while the children died.

Our family had been especially fortunate because none of our little ones became ill. Although Hovnan was only six years old, he seemed to realize what was going on. My youngest aunt, Hagenoush, who was with us, was carried off from the road by a zaptieh, who beat her terribly when she tried to resist him. When he had outraged her, he buried his knife in her breast and drove her back to us screaming with the fright and pain. I think I was never so discouraged as when we had treated Hagenoush and eased her pain.

News of the massacres and deportations had not yet reached all the villages we passed, as the road was little traveled. We came upon one settlement of Armenians where the women were at their wash tubs, in the public washing place, only partly clothed, as is the way in country villages in Turkey. Our guards surrounded the women at once and drove them, just as they were, into our party. Then they gathered the men, who did not know why they were molested until we told them. We rested on the road while the soldiers looted all the houses in that village. Then they set fire to it.

We were now in a country where there were many Turkish villages, as well as settlements of Kurds. We camped at night in a great circle, with the younger girls distributed for protection inside the circle as widely as possible. Each day young women were carried away to be sold to Turks who lived nearby, and at night the zaptiehs selected the most attractive women and outraged them.

The night after the Armenian village had been surprised, we had hardly more than made our camp when the captain of the soldiers ordered the men who had been taken from the village during the day to come before him, in a tent which had been pitched a little way off. The captain wanted their names, the soldiers explained. We had hoped these men would remain with us. There were seventy-two of them, and we felt much safer and encouraged with them among us. But we knew what the summons meant. The men knew, too, and so did their womenfolk.

Each man said good-by to his wife, or daughters, or mother, and other relatives who had been gathered in at the village. The captain's tent was just a white speck in the moonlight. Around it we made out the figures of soldiers and zaptiehs. The women clung to the men as long as they dared, then the men marched out in a little company. Our guards would not allow us to follow. We watched, hoping against hope.

Soon we saw a commotion. Screams echoed across to us. Figures ran out into the desert, with other figures in pursuit. Only the pursuers would return. Then it was quiet. The men were all dead.

That was the first time the officers had raised a tent. We wondered at their doing this, as usually they slept in the open after their nightly orgies with our girls. After that, we shuddered more than ever whenever we saw the soldiers put up a tent for the night.

After the massacre of the men, the soldiers who had participated came into the camp and, with those which had remained guarding us, went among us selecting women whose husbands had belonged to the more prosperous class and ordering them to go to the tent. The captain wished to question them, the soldiers said. They summoned my mother and many women who had been our neighbors or friends, until more than two hundred women whose husbands had been rich or well-to-do were gathered. With my mother my Aunt Mariam, whose husband had been a banker, was taken.

As soon as the women had arrived at the tent the captain told them they were summoned to give up the money they had brought with them, "for safe keeping from the Kurds," he said. The women knew their money would never be returned to them and that they would suffer terribly without it. They refused to surrender it, saying they had none. Then the zaptiehs fell upon them. They searched them all, first tearing off all their clothes.

One woman, who was the sister of the rich man, Garabed Tufenkjian, of Sivas, and who had been visiting in our city when the deportations began, was so mercilessly beaten she confessed at last that she had concealed some money in her person. She begged the soldiers to cease beating her that she might give it them. The soldiers shouted aloud with glee at this confession and recovered the money themselves, cutting her cruelly with their knives to make sure they had missed none.

The soldiers then searched each woman in this way. My Aunt Mariam was to become a mother. When the soldiers saw this, they threw her to the ground and ripped her open with their bayonets, thinking, in their ignorant way, she had hidden a great amount of money. They were so disappointed they fell upon the other women with renewed energy.

Of the two hundred or more who were subjected to this treatment, only a little group survived. When they crawled back into the camp and into the arms of their relatives, they had screamed so much they could not talk — they had lost their voices. My poor mother had given up all the money she had about her, but had not admitted that others of her family had more. She was bleeding from many cuts and bruises when she reached us, and fainted as soon as she saw Lusanne and me running to her. We carried her into the camp and used the last of our drinking water, which we had treasured from the day before, to bathe her wounds.

When the soldiers and zaptiehs had divided the money which they had taken, they came in among us again to pick out young women to take to the officers' tent. The moonlight was so bright none of us could conceal ourselves. Lusanne was sitting with the children, comforting them, while I had taken my turn at attending mother's wounds. A zaptieh caught her by the hair and pulled her to her feet.

"Spare me, my mother is dying — spare me!" Lusanne cried, but the zaptieh was merciless. He dragged her along. I could not

66

hold myself. I ran to Lusanne and caught hold of her, pleading with the zaptieh to release her. Lusanne resisted, too, and the zaptieh became enraged. With an oath he drew his knife and buried it in Lusanne's breast. The blade, as it fell, passed so close to me it cut the skin on my cheek, leaving the scar which I still have. Lusanne died in my arms. The zaptieh turned his attention to another girl he had noticed.

Mother had not seen — she was still too exhausted from her own sufferings. Aruciag and Hovnan, my little brother and sister, saw it all, however, and had run to where I stood dazed, with Lusanne's limp body in my arms. I laid her on the ground and wondered how I could tell mother.

A woman who had been standing near took my place at mother's side. I led the little ones away and asked another woman to keep them with her, then I returned to my sister's body. I could not make myself believe it. I counted on my fingers — father, mother, Paul, Lusanne, Aruciag, Sarah, Mardiros, Hovnan and my two aunts. With me that made eleven of us — eleven in our family. Then I counted father, Paul, Aunt Mariam, and now Lusanne — four already gone!

I cried over Lusanne a long time. Then I realized I must do something. I was afraid a sudden shock might kill mother, so I must have time, I knew, to prepare her. With the help of some other women, I carried Lusanne to the side of the camp and with our hands we dug her grave — just a shallow hole in the sand. I made a little cross from bits of wood we found after a long search, and laid it in her hands.

When morning came, mother had gathered her strength, with a tremendous effort, and was able to stand and walk. Some strong young women, offered to help carry her, even all day if necessary, if she could not walk. Mother insisted upon walking some of the time, though, leaning upon my shoulder.

She asked for Lusanne as soon as we began preparation to take up the day's march. I tried to make her believe Lusanne was further back in the company — "helping a sick lady," I said. But mother read my eyes — she knew I was trying to deceive her.

"Don't be afraid, little Aurora," she said to me, oh, so very gently; "don't be afraid to tell me whatever it is — have they stolen her?"

"They tried to take her," I said, "but — "

I stopped. Mother helped me again. "Did she die? Did they kill her? If they did, it was far better, my Aurora."

Then I could tell her. "They killed her — very quickly — her last words were that God was good to set her free."

We saw the zaptieh who killed Lusanne, during the day, and little Aruciag recognized him. "There is the man who killed my sister," she cried. Mother put her hands over her eyes and would not look at him.

We all were in great fear of what might happen to us at Hassan-Chelebi. Some of the young women who had been taken during the night to the tent of the officers reported that the officers had told them during the orgie that some great beys were coming from Sivas to meet us at Hassan-Chelebi, and that something was to be done about us there. We were afraid that meant that all our girls were to be stolen.

When the city loomed up before us, our young women began to tremble with dread, and many of them fell down, unable to walk, so great was their anguish. The soldiers whipped them up, though, and we were guided into the center of the town. Hundreds of our women were wholly nude, especially those who had been stripped and beaten when the soldiers robbed them. The zaptiehs would not allow them to cover themselves, seeming to take an especial delight in watching that those who were without clothes did not obtain garments from others. These poor women were compelled to walk through the streets of Hassan-Chelebi with their heads bowed with shame, while the Turkish residents jeered at them from windows and the roadside.

At the square, the Turkish officials from Sivas came out to look at us. Among them were Muamer Pasha, the cruel governor of Sivas; Mahir Effendi, his aide de camp; Tcherkess Kior Kassim, his chief hangman, who, we afterward learned, had superintended the massacre of 6,000 Armenian Christians at Tchamli-Bel gorge, near

Sivas; a captain of zaptiehs and a Hakim, or judge. Two of these officials were noted throughout Armenia — Muamer Pasha and his hangman, for their characteristic cruelties toward Christians.

After the officials had walked among us, closely surrounded by soldiers so that none could approach them, the Mudir, or under-mayor of the city, came with the police to get all boys over eight years of age. The police said the mayor had provided a school for them in a monastery, where they would be kept until their mothers had been permanently located somewhere and could send for them. Of course, we knew this was a false reason.

I greatly feared for Mardiros, but he was so small they did not take him. There must have been 500 boys with us who were between eight and fifteen, and these all were gathered.

The little fellows were taken to the mayor's palace. Then soldiers marched them away, all the little ones crying and screaming. We heard the cries a long time. When we arrived at Arabkir we were told by other refugees there that all the boys were killed as soon as they had crossed the hills into the valley just outside Hassan-Chelebi. The soldiers tied them in groups of ten and fifteen and then slew them with swords and bayonets. Refugees passing that way from Sivas saw their bodies on the road.

Before we left Hassan-Chelebi, Tcherkess Kior Kassim, the hangman, came among us, with a company of zaptiehs and picked out twelve very young girls — most of them between eight and twelve years old. The hangman was going soon to Constantinople, the soldiers said, and wanted young girls to sell to rich Turks of powerful families, among whom it is the custom to buy pretty girls of this age, whenever possible, and keep them in their harems until they mature. They are raised as Mohammedans and are later given to sons of their owners, or to powerful friends.

Just outside Hassan-Chelebi, which we left in the afternoon, we were joined by a party of 3,000 refugees from Sivas. They, too, were on their way to Arabkir, and had encamped outside the city to wait for us. Among them was a company of twenty Sisters of Grace. These dear Sisters, several of whom were Europeans, had been summoned at midnight from their beds by the Kaimakam, or under-governor. When the Turkish soldiers went for them, they were disrobed, sleeping. The soldiers would not permit them to dress, but took them as they were, barefooted and in their nightgowns.

They had managed, during the long days out of Sivas, to borrow other garments, but none had shoes and their feet were torn and bleeding. They were very delicate and gentle, and all had received their education in American or European schools. They had demanded exemption from the deportation under certain concessions made their convent by the Sultan, but the soldiers ignored their pleas.

Instead of arousing some slight respect upon the part of their guards because of their holy station, these Sisters had been subjected to the worst possible treatment. They told us that every night after their party left Sivas the soldiers and zaptiehs took them away from the party and violated them. They begged for death, but even this was refused them. Two of them, Sister Sarah and Sister Esther, who had come from America, had killed themselves. They had only their hands — no other weapons, and the torture and agonies they endured while taking their own lives were terrible.

The refugees from Sivas included the men. There were more than 25,000 Armenians in that city, and all were notified they were to be taken away. The party which joined ours was the first to be sent out. They had passed many groups of corpses along the road, they reported, the reminder of deportations from other cities.

When we arrived at Arabkir we were ordered to encamp at the edge of the city. Parties of exiles from many villages between Arabkir and Sivas already were there. Some of them still had their men and boys with them, others told us how their men had been killed along the route.

The Armenians of Arabkir itself were awaiting deportation, herded in a party of 8,000 or more, near where we halted. They had been waiting five days, and did not know what had happened to their homes in the city.

A special official came from Sivas to take charge of the deportations at Arabkir. With him came a company of zaptiehs. Halil Bey, a great military leader, with his staff, also was there, on his way to Constantinople where he was to take command of an army.

In the center of the city there was a large house which had been used by the prosperous Armenian shops. On the upper floors, were large rooms which had been gathering places. Already this house had come to be known as the Kasab-Khana — the "butcher-house" — for here the leading men of the city had been assembled and slain.

Shortly after the special official's arrival, soldiers summoned all the men still with the Sivas exiles, to a meeting with him on the Kasab-Khana. The men feared to go, but were told there would be no more cruelties now that high authority was represented. The men went, two thousands of them, and were killed as soon as they reached the Kasab-Khana. Soldiers were in, hiding on the lower floors and as the men gathered in the upper rooms, the doors were closed and the soldiers went about the slaughter. Men leaped out of the windows as fast as they could, but soldiers caught them on their bayonets.

The bodies were thrown out of the house later in the day. The next morning, they were still piled in the streets when the official called for the girls who had been attending the Christian colleges and schools at Sivas, and the Mission at Kotcheseur, an Armenian town near Sivas. There were two hundred of these girls, all of them members of the better families, and all between fifteen and twenty years old. The soldiers said the official had arranged for them to be sent under the care of missionaries to a school near the coast, where they would be protected.

The girls were summoned to the Kasab-Khana. It was then we learned, for the first time, what had happened to the men the day before. They stood in line but a few yards from the great piles of the bodies still lying in the street.

The official received them in a room on the upper floor of the house, which still bore the stains of blood on the walls and floors. He asked them to renounce Christ and accept Allah. Only a few agreed — these were taken away, where, I do not know. The rest were left in the room by the official and his staff. As soon as the officers had left the building, the soldiers poured into the room, sharing the girls among them. All day and night, soldiers went into and came out of the house. Nearly all the girls died. Those who were alive when the soldiers were weary were sent away under an escort of zaptiehs.

VI

RECRUITING FOR THE HAREMS OF
CONSTANTINOPLE

THE exiles from my city were kept in a camp outside Arabkir. On the third day the hills around us suddenly grew white with the figures of Aghja Daghi Kurds. They waited until nightfall then they rode down among us. There were hundreds of them, and when they were weary of searching the women for money, they began to gather up girls and young women.

I tried to conceal myself when a little party of the Kurds came near. But I was too late. They took me away, with a dozen other girls and young wives this band had caught. They carried us on their horses across the valley, over the hills and into the desert beyond. There they stripped us of what clothes still were on our bodies. With their long sticks they subdued the girls who were screaming, or who resisted them — beat them until their flesh was purple with flowing blood. My own heart was too full — thinking of my poor, wounded mother. I could not cry.

I was not even strong enough to fight them when they began to take the awful toll which the Turks and Kurds take from their women captives.

When the Kurds were tired of mistreating us, they hobbled us, still naked, to their horses. Each girl, with her hands tied behind her back, was tied by the feet to the end of a rope fastened around a horse's neck. Thus they left us — neither we nor the horses could escape.

I have often wondered since I came to America, where life is so different from that of my country, if any of the good people whom I meet could imagine the sufferings of that night while I lay in the darkness, my hands fastened and my feet haltered to the restless animal.

There seems to be so little of tragedy in this country — so little of real suffering. I can hardly believe yet, though I have been free so many months now, that there is a land where there is no punishment for believing in God.

When the dawn broke, the Kurds came out to untie their horses. It is characteristic of even the fiercest Kurds that their captives always are fed. The Kurds will rob and terribly mistreat their victims, especially the women of the Christians, but they will not steal their food. When their captives have no food they will even share with them. The Kurd is more of a child than the Turk, and nearly all the wickedness of these bandits of the desert is inspired by their Turkish masters.

When we had eaten of the bread and drank the water they brought for us, the Kurds lifted us upon their horses and galloped toward the north. There were more girls than Kurds, and we were shifted frequently that double burdens might be shared among the horses.

We did not know where we were being taken, nor to what. After many hours of riding, I was shifted to the care of a Kurd who — either because he was kinder or liked to talk — answered my pleading questions. He told me a great Pasha was at Egin, a city to the north, who had come down from Constantinople especially to take an interest in Armenian girls. This Pasha, the Kurd said, even paid money to have Christian girls who were healthy and pleasing brought before him.

Egin is on the banks of the Kara Su. From Erzindjan, Shabin Kara-Hissar and Niksar, large northern cities, thousands of Armenians had been brought to Egin. Here special bands of soldiers had been stationed to superintend the massacres of these Christians. All around the hills and plains outside the city, huge piles of corpses were still uncovered. We passed long ditches which had been dug by convicts released from Turkish prisons for that

74

purpose, and in which an attempt had been made to bury the bodies of the Armenians. But the convicts had been in such a hurry to get done the work for which they were to be given their liberty, that the legs and arms of men and women still stuck out from the sand which had been scraped over them.

There had been many rich Armenian families in Egin. It was the meeting place of the rich caravans from Samsoun, Trebizond and Marsovan, bound for Harpout and Diyarbekir. For many years, the Turkish residents and the Armenians had been good neighbors. When the first orders for the deportation and massacres reached Egin, the rich Armenian women ran to their Turkish friends, the wives of rich aghas and beys, and begged them for an intercession in their behalf. There was at that time an American missionary at the hospital in Egin who had been an interpreter attached to the American Embassy at Constantinople. He procured permission from the Kaimakam to appeal by the telegraph to the American Ambassador, Mr. Morgenthau, for the Christian residents of the city.

In the meantime, the rich Armenian women gave all their jewels and household silver and other valuables to the wives of the Turkish officials, and in this way obtained promises that they would not be molested until word had come from Constantinople. The American Ambassador secured from Talaat Bey, the Minister of the Interior, and Enver Pasha, the Minister of War, permission for the Armenians of Egin to remain undisturbed in their homes.

There was great rejoicing then among the Christians of Egin. A few days later, the first company of exiles from the villages to the west reached the city on their way to the south. They had walked for three days and had been cruelly mistreated by the zaptiehs guarding them. Their girls had been carried off and their young women had been the playthings of the soldiers. They were famished also for water and bread, and the Turks would give them none.

The Armenians of Egin were heart-stricken at the condition of these exiles, but they feared to help them. The refugees were camped at night in the city square. During the night, the zaptiehs and soldiers made free with the young women still among the exiles and their screams deepened the pity of the residents. In the

morning, the Armenian priest of the city could stand it no longer —
he went into the square with bread and water and prayers. The
Kaimakam had been watching for just such an occurrence!

He sent soldiers to bring the priest before him. He also sent for
twenty of the principal Armenian business men and had them
brought into the room. As soon as the Armenians arrived, his
soldiers set upon the priest and began to torture him, to pull out his
hair and twist his fingers and toes with pincers, which is a favorite
Turkish torture. The soldiers kept asking him as they twisted their
pincers:

"Did you not advise them to resist? Did you not take arms to
them concealed in bread?"

The priest screamed denials. The twenty men had been lined
up at one side of the room. In his trickery the Kaimakam had
stationed his soldiers at a distance from the Armenians. When the
torture of the priest continued and his screams died away into
groans, the Armenians could stand it no longer. They threw
themselves upon the torturers — not to assault them, but to beg
mercy for the holy man. Then the soldiers leaped upon them and
killed them all.

The Kaimakam reported to Constantinople that it was
impossible longer to obey the Ministry's orders to allow the
Armenians in Egin to remain — that they had revolted and attacked
his soldiers and that he had been forced to kill twenty of them.
Talaat Bey sent back the famous reply which now burns in the heart
of every Armenian in the world — no matter where he or she is —
for they all have heard of it. Talaat Bey's reply was:

"Whatever you do with Christians is amusing."

After this reply from Talaat Bey, the Kaimakam issued a
proclamation giving the Armenians of Egin just two hours to
prepare for deportation. The women besieged the officers and said
to them: "See, we have given our precious stones to your wives,
and we have given them many liras to give to you. Your wives
promised us protection, and we have done nothing to abuse your
confidence. Our men did not attack your soldiers in violence."

But the officers would only make light of them. "We would
have gotten your jewels and your money anyway," they replied.

In two hours they had assembled — all the Armenians in the city. The soldiers went among them and seized many of the young women. These they took to a Christian monastery just outside the city, where there were several other Armenian girls residing as pupils.

The Armenians had many donkeys and horse carriages. The mayor had told them they might travel with these. The soldiers tied the women in bunches of five, wrapped them tightly with ropes, and threw one bunch in each cart. Then they drove away the donkeys and horses and forced the men to draw these carts in which their womenfolk were bound. The soldiers would not let husbands or brothers or sons talk to their womenfolk, no matter how loudly they cried as the carts were pulled along.

An hour outside the city the soldiers killed the men. Then they untied the women and tormented them. After many hours, they killed the women who survived.

The Kaimakam sent his officers to the monastery where the young women were imprisoned. They took with them Turkish doctors, who examined the captives and selected the ones who were healthy and strong. Of these, the Turks required all who were maidens to stand apart from those who were not. The brides and young wives then were told they would be sent to Constantinople, to be sold there either as concubines or as slaves to farmer Turks. The maidens were told they might save their lives if they would forswear their religion and accept Mohammed. Some of them were so discouraged they agreed. An Imam said the rek'ah with them, and they were sent away into the hopeless land — to be wives or worse.

One maiden, the daughter of an Armenian leader who had been a deputy from that district to the Turkish Parliament, was especially pretty, and one of the officers wanted her for himself. He said to her:

"Your father, your mother, your brother and your two sisters have been killed. Your aunts and your uncles and your grandfather were killed. I wish to save you from the suffering they went through, and the unknown fate that will befall these girls who are Mohammedan now, and the known fate which will befall those who have been stubborn. Now, be a good Turkish girl and you shall be my wife — I will make you, not a concubine, but a wife, and you will live happily."

What the girl replied was so well remembered by the Turks who heard her that they told of it afterward ward among themselves until it was known through all the district. She looked quietly into the face of the Turkish officer and said:

"My father is not dead. My mother is not dead. My brother and sisters, and my uncle and aunt and grandfather are not dead. It may be true you have killed them, but they live in Heaven. I shall live with them. I would not be worthy of them if I proved untrue to their God and mine. Nor could I live in Heaven with them if I should marry a man I do not love. God would not like that. Do with me what you wish."

Soldiers took her away. No one knows what became of her. The other maidens who had refused to "turn" were given to soldiers to sell to aghas and beys. So there was none left alive of the Christians of Egin, except the little handful of girls in the harems of the rich — worse than dead.

When the Kurds carried me and the other girls they had stolen with me, into Egin they rode into the center of the city. We begged them to avoid the crowds of Turkish men and women on the streets because of our nakedness. They would not listen.

We were taken into the yard of a large building, which I think must have been a Government building. There we found, in pitiable condition, hundreds of other young Armenian women, who had been stolen from bands of exiles from the Erzinjdan and Sivas districts. Some had been there several days. Many were as unclothed as we were. Some had lost their minds and were raving. All were being held for an audience with the great Pasha, who had arrived at Egin only the night before.

This Pasha, we learned soon after our arrival, was the notorious Kiamil Pasha, of Constantinople. He was very old now, surely not less than eighty years, yet he carried himself very straight and firm. Once, many years before, he had been the governor of Aleppo and had become famous throughout the world for his cruelties to the Christians then. It was said he was responsible for the massacres of

1895, and that he had been removed from office once at the request of England, only to be honored in his retirement by appointment to a high post at Constantinople.

With Kiamil Pasha there was Boukhar-ed-Din Shakir Bey, who, I afterward learned, was an emissary of Talaat Bey and Enver Pasha.

A regiment of soldiers had come from Constantinople with Kiamil Pasha, and had camped just outside the city. This regiment later became known as the "Kasab Tabouri," the "butcher regiment," for it participated in the massacre of more than 50,000 of my people, under Kiamil Pasha's orders.

Kiamil Pasha and Boukhar-ed-Din-Shakir Bey came to the building where we were kept and sat behind a table in a great room. We were taken in twenty at a time. Even those who were nude were compelled to stand in the line which faced his table.

The pasha and the bey looked at us brutally when we stood before them. That which happened to those who went to the audience with me, was what happened to all the others.

"His Majesty the Sultan, in his kindness of heart, wishes to be merciful to you, who represent the girlhood of treacherous Armenia," said Boukhar-ed-Din-Shakir, while Kiamil looked at us silently. "You have been selected from many to receive the blessing of His Majesty's pity. You are to be taken to the great cities of Islam, where you will be placed under imperial protection in schools to be established for you, and where you may learn of those things which it is well for you to know, and forget the teachings of unbelievers. You will be kindly treated and given in marriage as opportunity arises into good Moslem homes, where your behavior will be the only measure of your content."

Those were his words, as truly as I can remember them. No girl answered him. We knew better than to put faith in Turkish promises, and we knew what even that promise implied — apostasy.

"Those of you who are willing to become Moslems will state their readiness," the bey continued.

Though I cannot understand them, I cannot blame those who gave way now. The Pasha and the Bey said nothing more. They just burned us with their cold, glittering eyes, and waited. The strain was too terrible. Almost half the girls fell upon their knees or into the arms of stronger girls, and cried that they would agree.

Boukhar-ed-Din-Shakir waved his hand toward the soldiers, who escorted or carried these girls into another room. We never heard of them again. Kiamil still looked coldly and silently at those of us who had refused. The Bey said not a word either, but raised his hand again. Then soldiers began to beat us with long, cruel whips.

We fell to the floor under the blows. The soldiers continued to beat us with slow, measured strokes — I can feel them now, those steady, cutting slashes with the whips the Turks use on convicts whom they bastinado to death. A girl screamed for mercy and shouted the name of Allah. They carried her into the other room. Another could not get the words out of her throat. She held out her arms toward the Pasha and the Bey, taking the blows from the whip on her hands and wrists until they saw that she had given in. Then she, too, was carried out. Others fainted, only to revive under the blows that did not stop.

Twice I lost consciousness. The second time, I did not come to until it was over and, with others who had remained true to our religion, had been left in the courtyard. I think there were more than four hundred young women in the yard when I first was taken into it. Not more than twenty-five were with me now — all the rest had been beaten into apostasy. No one can tell what became of them. It was said Kiamil and Boukhar-ed-Din Shakir sent more than a thousand Armenian girls to Kiamil's estates on the Bosphorus, where they were cared for until their prettiness had been recovered and their spirits completely broken, when they were distributed among the rich beys and pashas who were the political associates of Kiamil, Boukhar-ed-Din-Shakir Bey, and Djevdet Bey of Van.

We were kept in the courtyard four days, with nothing to eat but a bit of bread each day. Three of the young women died of their wounds. Often Turkish men and women would come to look into the yard and mock us. Turkish boys sometimes were allowed to throw stones at us.

On the fourth day we were taken out by zaptiehs to join a party of a thousand or more women and children who had arrived during the night from Baibourt. All the women in this party were middle-aged or very old, and the children were very small. What girls and young women were left when the party reached Egin, had been kept in the city for Kiamil and Boukhar-ed-Din-Shakir Bey to dispose of. The older boys had been stolen by Circassians. There were almost no babies, as these either had died when their mothers were stolen or had been killed by the soldiers.

With this party, we went seven hours from the city and were halted there to wait for larger parties of exiles from Sivas and Erzindjan, which were to meet at that point on the way to Diyarbekir.

Both these parties had to pass through Divrig Gorge, which was nearby. The exiles from Erzindjan never reached us. They were met at the gorge by the Kasab Tabouri, the butcher regiment, and all were killed. There were four thousand in the party. Just after this massacre was finished the exiles from Sivas came into the gorge from the other side.

The soldiers of the Kasab Tabouri were tired from their exertions in killing the 4,000 exiles from Erzindjan such a short time before, so they made sport out of the reception of those from Sivas, who numbered more than 11,000 men, women and children.

Part of the regiment stood in line around the bend of the gorge until the leaders of the Armenians came into view. Panic struck the exiles at once, and they turned to flee, despite their guards. But they found a portion of the regiment, which had been concealed, deploying behind them and cutting off their escape from the trap.

As the regiment closed in, thousands of the women, with their babies and children in their arms, scrambled up the cliffs on either side of the narrow pass, helped by their men folk, who remained on the road to fight with their hands and sticks against the armed soldiers.

But the zaptiehs who accompanied the party surrounded the base of the cliffs and kept the women from escaping. Then the Kasab Tabouri killed men until there were not enough left to resist them. Scores of men feigned death among the bodies of their friends, and thus escaped with their lives.

Part of the soldiers then scaled the cliffs to where the women were huddled. They took babies from the arms of mothers and threw them over the cliffs to comrades below, who caught as many as they could on their bayonets. When babies and little girls were all disposed of this way, the soldiers amused themselves awhile making women jump over — prodding them with bayonets, or beating them with gun barrels until the women, in desperation, jumped to save themselves. As they rolled down the base of the cliff, soldiers below hit them with heavy stones or held their bayonets so they would roll onto them. Many women scrambled to their feet after falling and these the soldiers forced to climb the cliffs again, only to be pushed back over.

The Kasab Tabouri kept up this sport until it was dark. They were under orders to pass the night at Tshar-Rahya, a village three hours from the gorge, so when darkness came and they were weary even of this game, they assembled and marched away singing, some with babies on their bayonets, others with an older child under their arms, greatly pleased with such a souvenir. Some salvaged a girl from the human debris and made her march along to unspeakable shame at the Tshar-Rahya barracks.

Only 300 of all the 11,000 exiles lived and were able to march under the scourging of the handful of zaptiehs who remained to guard them. They joined us where we had halted.

VII

MALATIA — THE CITY OF DEATH

SEVEN days after the massacre at Divrig Gorge, those of us who survived the cruelties of our guards along the way, saw just ahead of us the minarets of Malatia, one of the great converging points for the hundreds of thousands of deported Armenians on their way to the Syrian deserts which, by this time, I knew to be the destination of those who were permitted to live. When the minarets came into view, I was much excited by the hope that perhaps my mother's party might have reached there and halted, and that I might find her there.

When we drew close to the city, we passed along the road that countless other exiles had walked before. At the side of the road, in ridicule of the Crucifixion and as a warning to such Christian girls as lived to reach Malatia, the Turks had crucified on rough wooden crosses sixteen girls. I do not know how long the bodies had been there, but vultures already had gathered.

Each girl had been nailed alive upon her cross, great cruel spikes through her feet and hands. Only their hair, blown by the wind, covered their bodies. "See," said our guards with great satisfaction; "see what will happen to you in Malatia if you are not submissive."

In the vicinity of Malatia, and in the city itself, there were more than twenty thousand refugees waiting to be sent on. Kurds were camped outside in little bands, each with its "Claw chief," waiting to waylay and plunder the exiles. Arabs rode about the hills in the distance — outlaw bands, who swooped down upon the Christians in the night and stole the strongest of the women and girls for the harvesting in the fields. Turkish beys and aghas, with here and there a dignified pasha, rode out along the road to inspect each band of exiles as it approached the city, their cruel, sensual eyes trying to pierce the veils the younger girls wrapped about their faces to conceal their youth and prettiness.

From Sivas, Tokat, Egin, Erzindjan, Kerasun, Samsoun and countless smaller cities in the north, where the Armenians had had their homes for centuries, they had all been started toward Malatia. All the rivers in between were running red with blood; the valleys were great open graves in which thousands of bodies were left unburied; mountain passes were choked with the dead, and every rich Turk who kept a harem between the Black Sea and the River Tigris, had one or more, sometimes a score, of new concubines — Armenian girls who had been stolen for them along the road to this city.

I often wonder if the good people of America know what the Armenians are — their character. I sometimes fear Americans think of us as a nomad people or as people of a lower class. We are, indeed, different. My people were among the first converts to Christ. They are a noble race, and have a literature older than that of many other peoples in the world.

Very few Armenians are peasants. Nearly all are tradesmen, merchants, great and small, financiers, bankers or educators. In my city alone there were more than a score of business men or teachers who had received their education at American colleges. Hundreds had attended great European universities. My own education was received partly at the American college at Marsovan and partly from private tutors. Many Armenians are very wealthy. Few Turks are as fortunate in this respect as the great Armenian merchants.

Of the twenty thousand Christians herded in Malatia, in camps outside the city, in the public square or in houses set apart by the Turks for that purpose, I think much more than half were the members of well-to-do families, girls who had been educated either in Europe or in great Christian colleges at home, such as that at Marsovan, Sivas or Harpout, or in schools conducted by the Swiss,

84

the Americans, the English and the French. These girls had been taught music, literature and art.

I want to tell what happened to one group of school girls near Malatia, as it was told me by one of them.

At Kirk-Goz, a small city outside Malatia, there had been a German school, where young Armenian women from all over the district were sent to be taught by German teachers. The rule of the school was that the money received from the rich Armenian girls for their tuition was used in paying the expenses of poor girls. There were more than sixty pupils at this school when the attack on the Armenians began. As the school was under German protection, these girls considered themselves safe, and their families were happy to think they were protected. Aziz Bey, the Kaimakam, sent soldiers, however, with orders to bring all the girls into Malatia, to be deported or worse. Mme. Roth, the principal, refused to open the gates. She declared Eimen Effendi, the German consular agent in that district, would demand reparation if any attack on the school's pupils were made.

Mme. Roth — who was a German and old — herself, went to Malatia to consult Eimen Effendi. He told her Turkey was an ally of Germany, that Turkey declared Armenians to be obnoxious, and that Germany, therefore, must support the Sultan. He said the pupils would have to be surrendered. Then the soldiers took them away. Each girl was permitted to have a donkey, which the teachers bought in the city for them. They started west, to Mezre, where, the authorities promised, the girls would be taken care of in a dervish monastery.

Mme. Roth went, herself, before Aziz Bey and pleaded for the girls. She told him she was ashamed of being a German since Eimen Effendi had allowed such a horrible thing to be perpetrated with the consent of Germany. She offered the Bey all her personal possessions, all the money she had with her at Kirk-Goz, if he would return the girl pupils and allow her to keep them with her. Mme. Roth was very wealthy. She had more than 1,000 liras, and jewels worth much more. Aziz Bey accepted the bribe and sent her, with an escort of soldiers, after the young women.

85

Two days later Mme. Roth and her escort approached the crossing of the river Tokma-Su, at the little village Keumer-Khan. There were tracks on the plain which showed the party they sought had passed that way but a little while before. Suddenly down the road toward them came an unclothed girl, running madly and screaming in terror. When she came near Mme. Roth and recognized her, the girl cried, "Teacher, teacher, save me! Save me!"

The girl, whose name was Martha, and whose parents were rich people of Zeitoun, threw herself on the ground at her teacher's feet and clasped them. "Save me! Save me!" she continued to scream. Mme. Roth gave her drops of brandy from a bottle she had carried with her, and tried to quiet her. Two zaptiehs from the guard which the bey had sent with the school girls came running up. When Martha saw them, she went mad again and became unconscious. The zaptiehs tried to take possession of her limp body, but Mme. Roth defied them. Her escort persuaded the zaptiehs to go away. When Mme. Roth knelt again by the girl, she was dead. Marks on her body and bruises and wounds and her torn hair were evidences of the struggle she had made to save herself.

Mme. Roth hurried on. She heard more screams as she neared the river banks. She came upon two zaptiehs, sitting on the sand, prodding with a pointed stick the bare shoulders of a girl whom they had buried in the earth above her elbows. This was a favorite pastime of the zaptiehs of the Euphrates provinces. They had commanded the girl to submit to them quietly and she had fought them. To punish her and break her spirit, they buried her that way and tortured her. She screamed with pain and fright, and this amused them greatly. When they wished the zaptiehs would take her out, and then bury her again. It was from such torture as this Martha had escaped.

The soldiers of Mme. Roth's escort rescued the girl, at her command. Mme. Roth left her with three soldiers and crossed the river. She could hear screams from the other side. At once zaptiehs on the raft taking them across the river broke into a loud guffaw. The oarsmen steered the raft so as to escape two floating objects, and it was these which amused them. Mme. Roth saw the bodies of two of her girls floating down the river from where the screams came.

"Look — look there," shouted a laughing zaptieh; "two more Christians whom their Christ forgot!" On the other side Mme. Roth found all who were left of her sixty or more pupils — only seventeen. Their lives were saved only because the zaptiehs had become weary. They were, too, the least pretty of the original party. Mme. Roth took them all back to Malatia, where the Kaimakam insisted that she house them. They were living there in constant fear of being taken away again when I was taken from the city.

It was said by those who knew, that Mme. Roth refused to receive Eimen Effendi when he called upon her after her return with her surviving pupils. It is said she sent word to him that she was no longer German, and would ask no protection except that which she could buy with gold liras as long as she could obtain them from her relatives.

In every open space in the city and in every empty building Armenian refugees were camped, hungry, footsore and dying, with little food or water. In all our company, there were not ten loaves of bread when we entered the city. When we asked at the wells of Turks for water we were spat at, and if soldiers were near, the Turks would call them to drive us away. Each day, thousands of the refugees were taken away, and each day thousands of others arrived from the north.

Inside the city, there was no attempt to care for the arriving exiles. Some of the men in our party finally led the way to a great building which had been a barracks, but in which many thousands of Christians had taken refuge. We seldom ventured out on the streets, for Turkish boys and Kurds and Arabs thronged the streets and threw stones or sticks at us, or, in the case of girls as young as I, carried them into Turkish shops or low houses, and there outraged them.

When we had passed the second day in Malatia, I could rest no longer without seeking my mother — hoping that she and the Armenians of Tchemesh-Gedzak might be among the other refugees. I went into the street at night and went from place to place where exiles were herded. Nowhere could I find familiar faces — people from my own city.

When morning came, I could not find my way back to the building I had left. Morning comes quickly in the midst of the plains, and soon it was light, and I was in a part of the city where there were no exiles. The streets of Malatia are very narrow, and there are few byways. My bare feet were tired from walking all night on cobblestones and pavements. I felt very tired — not as if I really were but little over fourteen. I knew I would soon be carried into one of these Turkish houses and lost, perhaps forever, if soldiers or gendarmes should catch me at large. I hid in a little areaway.

Suddenly I realized that I was hugging the walls of a house over which hung the American flag. A feeling of relief came over me. The American flag is very beautiful to the eyes of all Armenians! For many years it has been to my people the promise of peace and happiness. We had heard so much of the wonderful country it represented. Armenia always has thought of the United States as a friend ever ready to help her.

When the street was clear, I left my hiding place and went to the door of the house. I rapped, but Turks entered the street just then and spied me. They were citizens, not soldiers, but they shouted and started to run at me, recognizing me perhaps from the bits of garments which I had managed to gather to cover my body, as an Armenian.

I screamed and pushed at the door. It opened, and I found myself in the arms of a woman who was hurrying to let me in.

I was too frightened to explain. The Turks were at the door. I thought I would be carried away. One of them pushed himself inside the door. Another followed, and they reached out their hands to take me. The woman, who was not Turkish, stepped in front of me. "What do you want? — Why are you here?" she asked in Turkish. "The girl — we want her. She has escaped," they said.

The woman startled me by refusing to allow me to be taken. She told the Turks they had no authority. When the men motioned as if to take me by force, she stepped in front of me and told them to remember that I was her guest. One of the men said:

"The girl is an Armenian. She has run away from the rest of her people. She has no right to be at large in the city. The Kaimakam has ordered citizens to take into custody all Christians found outside quarters set aside for them to rest in while halting on their way past the city."

"Your Kaimakam's orders have nothing to do with me. I shall protect the girl. You dare not harm an American!" said my new friend. The Turks, grumbling among themselves, and threatening vengeance, went out.

The young woman told me she was Miss McLaine, an American missionary. The house was the home of the American consul at Malatia, but he had taken his wife, who was ill, to Harpout. Miss McLaine kept the flag flying while they were gone. She had tried to persuade the officials to be less cruel to the refugees, but could do very little. She had been a pupil of Dr. Clarence Ussher, the noted American missionary surgeon, of New York, and Mrs. Ussher, both of whom were famous throughout Armenia for their kindness to our people during the massacres at Van. Mrs. Ussher lost her life at Van.

Late that day a squad of soldiers came from the Kaimakam to the consul's house and demanded that I be given up. Miss McLaine again refused to surrender me. The soldiers declared they had orders to take me by force. Miss McLaine asked that they take her to the Kaimakam that she might ask his protection for me. To this the soldiers agreed, and I was left alone in the house.

When Miss McLaine returned, she was crying. The soldiers returned with her. The Kaimakam had said I must rejoin the exiles, but that I might be taken to a house where a large company of women who had embraced Mohammedanism were confined, with their children. This company, the mayor said, was to be protected until they reached a place selected by the government.

So Miss McLaine could do nothing more. She kissed me, and the soldiers led me away to the house where the apostatized women with their children were quartered.

These apostatized Armenians were nearly all women from small cities between Malatia and Sivas. None of them really had given up Christianity, but they thought they were doing right, as nearly all the women were the mothers of small children who were with them. They wanted to save the lives of their little ones. They did not know what was to become of them, but the beys had promised they would be taken care of by the government.

This party of exiles was fed by the Turks — bread, water and coarse cakes. We were not allowed out of the house, but the Turks did not bother us. I soon had occasion to realize that the Kaimakam really had given me at least some protection when he allowed me to join this party.

In some of the companies waiting in Malatia, the men had not been killed. One day, the soldiers gathered all of these into one big party. The mayor wanted them to register, the soldiers said, so allotments of land could be made them at their destination in the south. So earnest were the soldiers the men believed them. Many went without even putting on their coats. They were marched to the building in which I had first been quartered, and from which other refugees had been taken out the night before.

Almost 3,000 men were thus assembled. Outside, soldiers took up their station at the doors and windows. Other soldiers then robbed the men of their money and valuables — such as they had saved from Kurds along the road, and then began killing them. When bodies had piled so high the soldiers could not reach survivors without stumbling in blood, then they used their rifles, and killed the remainder with bullets.

That afternoon, soldiers visited all the camps of refugees and took children more than five years old. I think there must have been eight or nine thousands of these. The soldiers came even to the house in which I was with the "turned" Armenians, and despite the promises of the mayor, took all our boys and girls. When mothers clung to their little ones and begged for them, the soldiers beat them off. "If they die now, your God won't be troubled by having to look after them till they grow up," the soldiers said — and always with a brutal laugh.

They took the children to the edge of the city, where a band of Aghja Daghi Kurds was waiting. Here the soldiers gave the children into the keeping of the Kurds, who drove them off toward the Tokma River, just outside the city. The Kurds drove the little ones like a flock of sheep. At the river banks, the boys were thrown into the river. The girls were taken to Turkish cities, to be raised as Mohammedans

VIII

IN THE HAREM OF HADJI GHAFOUR

AFTER the massacre of the men all the exiles waiting in Malatia were told to prepare for the road again. We were assembled outside the city early one morning. Only women and some children, with here and there an old man, were left. We were told we were to be taken to Diyarbekir, a hundred miles across the country. Very few had hopes of surviving this stage of the journey, as the country was thickly dotted with Turkish, Circassian and Kurdish villages, and inhabited by most fanatical Moslems. Civilians were more cruel to the deportees along the roads between the larger cities, than the soldiers. Some of the treatment suffered by our people from these fanatical residents of small towns was such that I cannot even write of it.

When the column was formed, outside Malatia, it was made up of fifteen thousand women, young and old. Very few had any personal belongings. Few had food. Many had managed to hold onto money, however, and these were ready to share what they had with those who had none. Money was the only surety of enough food to sustain life on the long walk, and the only hope of protection against a zaptieh's lust for killing.

The company of apostates which I had been permitted to join was placed at the head of the column, with a special guard of soldiers. Zaptiehs guarded the other companies, but there were very few assigned. Most of the zaptiehs in that district had been placed in the Mesopotamian armies. My party of apostates, of which there were about two hundred, was the best guarded. The others were wholly at the mercy of Kurds and villagers.

It was now late in June, and very hot. Scores of aged women dropped to the ground, prostrated by heat and famished for water, of which there was only that which we could beg from farmers along the way. The mother of two girls in my party, who, with her daughters, already had walked a hundred miles into Malatia, was beaten because she fell behind. She fell to the ground and could not get up. The soldiers would not let us revive her. Her two daughters could only give her a farewell kiss and leave her by the roadside.

One of these two girls was a bride — a widowed bride. She had seen her husband and father killed in the town of Kangai, on the Sivas road, and when the Kurds were about to kill her mother because she was old, she begged a Turkish officer, who was nearby, to save her. The officer had asked her if she would renounce her religion to save her mother, and she consented — she and her younger sister.

The sisters walked on with their arms about each other. They dared not even look around to where their mother lay upon the ground. When we could hear the woman's moans no longer, I walked over to them and asked them to let me stay near them. I knew how they must feel. I wondered if my own mother and my little brothers and sisters had lived. A soldier in Malatia had told me exiles from Tchemesh-Gedzak had passed through there weeks before and had gone, as we were going, toward Diyarbekir. Perhaps, he said, they might still be there when we arrived — if we ever did.

A few hours outside the city we were halted. We were much concerned by this, as such incidents usually meant new troubles. This time was no exception. As soon as we stopped, villagers flocked down upon us and began to rob us.

Just before sundown a loud cry went up. We looked to the east, where there was a wide pass through the hills, and saw a band of horsemen riding down upon us. They were Kurds, as we could tell from the way they rode. The villagers shouted — "It is Kerim Bey, the friend of Djebbar. It is well for us to scatter!" They then scrambled back into the hills, afraid, it seemed, the Kurd chieftain would not welcome their foraging among his prospective victims.

To say that Kerim Bey was "a friend of Djebbar" explained his coming with his band. Djebbar Effendi was the military commandant of the district, sent by the government at Constantinople to oppress Armenians during the deportations. His word was law, and always it was a cruel word. Kerim Bey was the most feared of the Kurd chiefs — he and Musa Bey. Both were of the Aghja Daghi Kurds. Kerim Bey and his band ruled the countryside, and frequently revolted against the Turks. To keep him as an ally Djebbar Effendi had given into his keeping many companies of exiled Armenians sent from Malatia to Diyarbekir and beyond.

There were hundreds of horsemen in Kerim's band. They had ridden far and were tired, too tired to take up the march in the moonlight, but not too tired to begin at once the nightly revels which kept us terrorized for so many days after. Scarcely had they hobbled their horses in little groups that stretched along the side of the column when they began to collect their toll. Screams and cries for mercy and the groans of mothers and sisters filled the night.

I saw terrible things that night which I cannot tell. When I see them in my dreams now I scream, so even though I am safe in America, my nights are not peaceful. A group of these Kurds so cruelly tortured one young woman that women who were nearby became crazed and rushed in a body at the men to save the girl from more misery. For a moment the Kurds were trampled under the feet of the maddened women, and the girl was hurried away.

When they recovered, the Kurds drew their long, sharp knives and set upon the brave women and killed them all. I think there must have been fifty of them. They piled their bodies together and set fire to their clothes. While some fanned the blaze, others searched for the girl who had been rescued, but they could not find her. So, baffled in this, they caught another girl and carried her to the flaming pile and threw her upon it. When she tried to escape, they threw her back until she was burned to death.

When the Kurds approached my party of apostates, the soldiers with us turned them away. "You may do as you wish with the others — these are protected," said the Turkish officer in charge. But this same officer was not content to be only a spectator while the Kurds were reveling.

Five soldiers came from his tent and sought a young woman they thought would please their chief. They tore aside the veils of women whose forms suggested they might be young, until they came upon a girl from the town of Derenda, toward Sivas. She was very pretty, but one of the soldiers, when they were dragging her off, recognized her. "Kah!" he grunted to his comrades. "This one will not do. She is no longer a maid!" They pushed her aside and sought further. But each girl they laid their hands on after that cried to them, "I, too, am not a virgin!" Each one was given a blow and thrust aside when she claimed to have been already shamed.

Soon the soldiers saw they were being cheated of the choicest prey. They turned upon some older women and seized three. One of them they forced to her knees and two of the soldiers held her head back between their hands until her face was turned to the stars. Another soldier pressed his thumbs upon her eyeballs, and said:

"If there be no virgin among you, then by Allah's will this woman's eyes come out!"

There was a cry of horror, then a shriek. A girl who must have been of my own age, and whom I had often noticed because her hair was so much lighter than that of nearly all Armenian girls, threw herself, screaming, upon the ground at the soldiers' feet. Winding her hands about the legs of the soldier whose thumbs were pressing against the woman's eyes, she cried:

"My mother! my mother! Spare her — here I am — I am still a maid!"

The soldiers seized the girl, guffawing loudly at the success of their plan. As they lifted her between them, she flung out her hands toward the woman, who had fallen in a heap when the soldiers released her. "Mother," the girl screamed, "kiss me — kiss me!"

The poor woman struggled to her feet and reached out her arms, but her eyes were hurt and she could not see. The girl begged the soldiers to carry her to her mother. "I will go — I will go, and be willing — but let me kiss my mother!" she cried. But the soldiers hurried her away.

The mother stood, leaning on those who crowded close to comfort her. Then, suddenly, she drooped and sank to the ground. When we bent over her, she was dead. We sat by the body until the daughter came back — after the moon had crossed the sky, and it must have been midnight. The girl hid her face when she came near, until she could bury it in her mother's shawl. She sat by the body until morning, when we took up our march again.

Every night such things happened.

Other parties along that road had fared the same. Sometimes I counted the bodies of exiles who had preceded us until I could count no longer. They lay at the roadside, where their guards had left them, for miles.

On the eleventh day, we came to Shiro, the Turkish city where caravans for Damascus spend the night in a large khan and then turn southward. There are even more caravans now than there used to be, for now they travel only to the Damascus railway and then return. Shiro is the home of many Turks, who profit from traders, or who have retired from posts of power and profit at Constantinople. It is not a large town, but more a settlement of wealthy aghas.

We camped outside this little city. Early the next morning, military officers came out. Kerim Bey met them, and there was a short conference. Then the Kurds began to gather the prettiest girls. They tore them from their relatives and half dragged, half carried them to where guards were placed to take charge of them.

All morning the Kurds carried young women away until more than a hundred had been accepted by the officer from the city. Then the apostates were ordered to join these weeping girls, and we were marched into the town.

The narrow streets were crowded with Turks and Arabs. They hooted at us, and made cruel jests as we passed. Among the apostates were many old women, whose daughters had sworn to be Mohammedans to save them. When the crowds saw these, they laughed with ridicule. Once the citizens swooped down upon the party and, unhindered by our guards, seized four of the older women, stripped off their clothing and carried them away on their shoulders, shouting in great glee. We never heard what became of these. I think they were just tossed about by the crowd until they died.

We were taken to a house which we soon learned was the residence of Hadji Ghafour, one of the largest houses in the city. Only devout Moslems who have made the pilgrimage to Mecca may be called "Hadji." Hadji Ghafour was looked up to as one of the most religious of men.

In the house of Hadji Ghafour we were crowded into a large room, with bare stone walls, where camels and dromedaries were often quartered overnight.

Hadji Ghafour came into the room, accompanied by soldiers. We of the apostate party had been put into one corner with Kurds to watch us. Hadji Ghafour gave an order to his servants and they separated the most pleasing girls and younger women from the others. Of these, with me among them, there were only thirty. We were taken out of the room and into another, not so large, on another floor of the house. The fate of those who were not satisfactory to Hadji Ghafour I never learned. A soldier told one of us they were allowed to rejoin the deportation parties.

Those of us who had been chosen were taken to the hammam, or bath chamber, and garments were brought for those whose clothes were frayed or, as it was with some, who had almost none at all. Turkish women and negro slave girls watched us in the bath and locked us up again.

At the end of an hour, we heard steps. The door was opened and a huge black slave, with other negroes behind him, summoned us. Frightened and too cowed to ask questions or hold back, we followed the slave through halls and up stairways, until we came to a huge rug-strewn chamber, brilliantly lighted with lamps and candles. On divans heavy with cushions, at one side of the room, sat Hadji Ghafour and a group of other Turks who were of his class, all middle aged or older, none with a kindly face.

Those of us who had been taken from the apostatized party stood to one side, while a servant said, to the others:

"It is the will of Hadji Ghafour, whose house has given you refuge, that you repay his kindness in saving you from the dangers that confront your people, by repenting of your unbelief and accept the grace of Islam."

The Turks made sounds of approval, and a turbaned Khateeb, or priest of the mosque, entered the chamber, with an attendant who carried the prayer rug. Behind him was a negro servant carrying a whip of bull's hide. The prayer rug was spread, and the Khateeb waited.

The Turks pointed to a shrinking girl and the servants pulled her out. "What say you?" the officer asked. "I belong to Christ — in His keeping I must remain," the girl replied. The negro's whip fell across her shoulders. When she screamed for mercy, the Khateeb bared his feet, stepped upon the prayer rug and turned to Mecca. "Allah is most great; there is no God but Allah!" his voice droned. The negro flung the girl onto the carpet. He held his cruel whip ready to strike again if she did not quickly kneel. Her face also turned to Mecca as she stumbled to her knees. Her flesh already was torn and bleeding. Terror of the whip was in her heart. To escape it, she could only say the rek'ah — "There is no God but Allah and Mohammed is his prophet."

When the last one had recited the sacrilegious creed the Khateeb folded the prayer rug and left the room. Hadji Ghafour, smiling now, ordered us all to stand before his guests again. All were apostates now except me, whom the Turks thought had previously taken the oath, else I would not have been in the party which I had joined. The law as well as Hadji Ghafour's piousness allowed them to do with us now as they chose.

One by one they selected us, according to their fancies — Hadji Ghafour first, and then his guests. How they had arranged the order of choice I do not know, but they had agreed among themselves. There were five or six girls for each of the Turks. I was among those ordered aside for Hadji Ghafour, who had also chosen the two daughters who had been compelled to leave their mother dying on the Sivas road.

The two sisters had been very quiet all that day. They had spoken but little to any of the rest of us since we were taken into the house of Hadji Ghafour. Nor had they cried — afterwards I

98

remembered how their faces that day seemed to be bright with a great courage.

The girls chosen by the guests of Hadji Ghafour were taken away in separate groups to the houses of those who claimed their bodies. When these guests and their captives had gone, Hadji Ghafour again summoned us. It was one of the sisters, the elder, to whom he spoke first. His words were terrible. He asked her, oh, so cruelly low and soft, if she were willing to belong to him, body and soul, to live contented in his house, to be obedient and — affectionate in her submission.

The girl waited not an instant. "I had renounced my God to save my mother, but it availed me nothing. Her life was taken. I have given myself to God — and I will not betray Him again!"

Hadji Ghafour motioned to his negro slave, who caught the girl in his arms and carried her out of the room. Her sister had been standing near her. Hadji Ghafour's eyes fell upon her next.

"And you, my little one," he said, just as low and soft. And he repeated the questions to her he had spoken to her sister. She spoke softly, too — softer than had her sister, yet just as firmly. "She was my sister. With her I saw my mother die, and now you have taken her. You may kill me also, but I will never submit to you."

Those of us who watched, looked with terror at Hadji Ghafour. This time his eyes narrowed and glittered. "You have spoken well, my little one," he said, still so gently he might have been speaking to a beloved daughter. "Perhaps I had better kill you as a warning to my other little ones."

The negro with the whip stood near. Hadji Ghafour did not even speak to him — just motioned with his hands. Two other servants sprang forward. Quickly they stripped the girl of her clothes. And then the whip fell upon her naked body.

I shut my eyes so I could not see, but I could not shut out the sound of the whip cutting into the flesh, again and again, until I lost count. Even when the girl screamed no more and her moans died away the whip did not stop for a long time. Then suddenly I realized the blows had ceased. I opened my eyes and saw one of the servants lifting the girl's body from the floor. He held her by the waist, and her arms and bleeding legs hung limp. She was dead.

None of us had courage after that. We gave Hadji Ghafour our promises. We were taken out another door, this time to the women's apartments, where women of the household were waiting to receive us.

IX

THE RAID ON THE MONASTERY

THE women of the haremlik had retired, except the three who awaited our coming. These took us through a long, narrow corridor, lit only by a single lamp, to a separate wing of the house. Through a curtained doorway we entered a series of small stone-floored rooms, in which women were sleeping. At last we came to a wooden door, which one of the women opened, pushing us through. One of them lit a taper.

WAITING THEY KNOW NOT WHAT
Armenians of a prosperous city assembled in front of a government building, by order of the authorities. They are waiting to be deported. Just outside the city they were massacred.

The room was barren, with not even a window. On the floor was a row of sleeping rugs, but there were neither cushions nor pillows. The women told us to remove our clothing, and took it from us as we obeyed. Without another word the women left us, taking the taper with them and locking the door.

Through the long night we waited — for what we did not know. We were afraid to sleep, even if we could.

We knew morning had come when we heard the faint call to prayer from some neighboring minaret. Soon the haremlik was astir. We trembled as we waited for the door to open.

It was a big negro who finally swung it wide, letting into the room the light from the windows that opened from the other rooms of the haremlik. One of the servant women who had received us the night before entered after him.

For each of us the woman brought an entareh, or Turkish house dress, and slippers and stockings. The dresses were of satin and linen, but very plain. Though I wanted something with which to cover myself, I could not help shrinking from the hated Turkish dresses. The woman saw me and seemed to understand.

"You will have prettier things after a while — after your betrothal!"

After my betrothal!

When we had dressed, with the aid of the woman, she ordered us to follow the negro. "What you will see now, according to the desire of Hadji Ghafour, will serve to guide your conduct in the haremlik," the woman said.

The slave led us through a smaller room into a large chamber, in which were gathered many excited women crowded about a window.

At the window-sill the slave peered out and then ordered us to draw nearer. The window opened upon a wide court. Across the court were many small windows. For a moment I saw nothing but the bleak stone wall. Then my eyes lifted to a window higher up. I shrieked and recoiled. The dead body of the elder sister of the girl who had been beaten to death, the one who had been carried away when she defied Hadji Ghafour, was hanging by its feet from a rope attached to the window-sill. The girl's arms had been tied behind her back and now hung away from her body. Her hair was hanging from her swaying head. A bandage, still tied over her mouth, had muffled her screams.

One of the girls with me, Lusaper, who had cried all night, fell to her knees and became hysterical. The slave lifted her and tried to make her look again. When he saw she was half mad, he carried her to a couch at the other side of the room and two little negro slave girls immediately began to comfort her. Other women crowded around her, too. The slave left us then, as did the woman servant who had been with us.

The women of the haremlik seemed to want to be very kind. The Turkish women were older than the apostate women. Hadji Ghafour's two wives were not among them, as their apartments were elsewhere, and I do not know what the relationship of the other women to him was, whether as concubines or relatives. Nearly all the younger women were Armenian girls who had been stolen. They were very sorry for us.

Food was brought in this chamber, and we ate together. Already I had made up my mind to be as brave as I could and to hope and pray that I might be delivered from that house.

All the Armenian girls in the haremlik had at one time passed through just such experiences as had been ours the night before in the presence of Hadji Ghafour. There were eight of them, and all had apostatized with the hope of saving relatives, only to be taken to Hadji Ghafour's house upon their arrival at Geulik. Only one of them knew what had become of her family. This one had seen her mother killed and her sister taken by the Kurds on the road from Malatia.

Four days I remained in the haremlik without being summoned by Hadji Ghafour. On the third day, one of the other of the "new" girls came back to us in the morning, quiet and ashamed, with her eyes downcast. That same day the harem slaves took away her plain entareh and gave her a richly embroidered dress. Such was the sign of her having been "betrothed."

We were not allowed outside the haremlik. Each night we were compelled to say the Mohammedan prayers. I learned to say them aloud and translate them in my mind into the words of Christian

103

prayers. The head servant of the haremlik, an elderly Turkish woman, who was as kind to us as she could be, took occasion every day to warn us that if we wished to live and be happy, we must be pleasing to Hadji Ghafour. Other women told us of girls who had come into the harem, never to appear again after their "betrothal" to the master. When these things were spoken of, we could not help thinking of the body we saw hanging from the window across the court — that was Hadji Ghafour's way of teaching us to be submissive.

We were not put in the dark, windowless room again. Once one of Hadji Ghafour's wives came into the harem to see us. She was middle-aged, and from Bagdad. She once had been very beautiful, I think, but seemed to be cruel and without affection. She had us brought before her and questioned each one of us about our experiences in the deportations. She seemed to want to trap us into admissions that we had not truly become Mohammedans.

Among the Armenian girls in the harem, was one who came from Perri, a village between my own city and Harpout. During the nights, she told me of the massacres in her village, and how the Turks had spared her because she acccpted Islam, until they reached Malatia. There she had been stolen, taken first to the home of a bey and then sent with other Armenian girls to Geulik. She, too, had been taken straight to the house of Hadji Ghafour. She had gone through with her "betrothal," and had found some favor in the eyes of the Turk.

This little girl was Arousiag Vartessarian, whose father, Ohannes, had owned much land. She had been educated at Constantinople. In Constantinople she learned of the American, Mr. Cleveland Dodge, of New York, who has done so much for education in Turkey. Since I have come to America, I have learned that this same Mr. Cleveland Dodge is the best friend the Armenians have in all the world.

Arousiag was secretly Christian still. But she did not hope ever to escape from the harem. She told me Hadji Ghafour kept Armenian girls only until he had tired of them or until prettier ones were available. Then he sent them to his friends, or to be sold to Turkish farmers. She had tried to please him, so she would not be sold into an even worse state, for sometimes a girl who falls into the slave market will be sold into a public house for soldiers and zaptiehs.

On the evening of the fifth day, my heart sank and my knees grew weak when a little negro slave girl came to tell me Hadji Ghafour had sent for me.

The servant women gathered around me, each professing not to understand why I was not elated. Only when my tears fell did they cease their jesting at the arrival — "at last," they said, of the hour of my supreme torture — my "good fortune" they called it.

While I was being dressed, I closed my eyes and prayed — not to be saved, for that was too late, but for strength and for the joy of knowing that God would be watching over me. One of the harem women walked with me down the narrow corridor and through the door I had not passed since I left Hadji Ghafour's presence five days before.

The lights of many lamps glowed in the room. Just inside the door the big negro was waiting. Across, on his cushions, with his nargilleh on the floor beside him, sat Hadji Ghafour. His eyes were full upon me when I stopped at the sound of the door closing behind me.

He motioned for me to approach and sit upon a cushion at his feet. Involuntarily I shrank back and threw my hands before my eyes. An instant later I felt the negro's hand gripping my arm. I tried to hold back and I tried to gather courage to go forward — I knew my hopes of a happier future depended upon my submission.

The negro tightened his grip. Under his breath he murmured, "Be a good little one. You will be the better for it." I could not look up, but I went and sat upon the cushion at Hadji Ghafour's feet!

It is needless to say more of that terrible night!

To Arousiag I confided the next day that I must, somehow, escape from Hadji Ghafour's house. To remain meant more tortures and lessened such chance as there might be that I would find my mother at Diyarbekir, where refugees with money were allowed by the Vali to remain just outside the city — provided they paid liberally for the privilege. When their money was gone, they were sent away with other exiles into the Syrian desert.

I had tried to coax Hadji Ghafour to send messengers to Diyarbekir to rescue my family if they could be found there, or to learn what had become of them. He would not grant me this favor. "You are a Turkish girl now," he said, "and you must forget all past associations with unbelievers."

Arousiag feared for me the consequences of my being caught in an attempt to escape. Captives who had tried to run away before had been sold into the public houses, where they soon died. When I had made her understand, though, that I would risk anything rather than remain in Hadji Ghafour's house, she promised to help me. It was then she told me, when we were alone in our couches that night, that to the west, across the plains, toward the Euphrates, was a monastery, founded ages ago by Roman Catholic Dominican Fathers, who came into Armenia as missionaries. During all the centuries Armenian religious refugees had been received in this monastery, Arousiag told me, and from there many teachers were sent into Syria and even to Kurdistan.

A man from Albustan, who really was an Armenian Derder, or priest, but who was disguised as a Turk and making his way to the Caucasus, where he hoped to get aid for the exiles from the Russians, had told Arousiag of the monastery while she was being kept in Malatia. Many Armenian girls had found safety there, the Derder had said, as the Fathers in the monastery had not been molested, and their refuge was far off the track of the companies of deported Christians. Many years ago, the Derder told Arousiag, the monastery Fathers had saved the life of a famous chieftain, and there were legends about it which kept the Kurds from attacking the monastery. For some reasons the Turks had not molested it, either.

Arousiag confided to me that she had often planned to escape from the house and try to go alone to the monastery. There, she was sure, there would be safety — for a time at least. But each time her courage deserted her. Now she was willing to make the effort, since I, too, would rather risk everything than remain a victim of Hadji Ghafour.

The windows of the sleeping apartments were high, and were not barred, as they opened only into a courtyard. Arousiag knew of a passageway from the courtyard into the divan-khane, or reception chamber, which opened onto the street. Often the servants of the haremlik went into the street through this passageway.

A night came when Hadji Ghafour sent early for the girl he desired. It was long before the haremlik's retiring hour. Arousiag and I slipped away and let ourselves down from a window into the courtyard. We hurried through the divan-khane and into the streets. We had veiled ourselves, and, with Turkish slippers, we were mistaken for Turkish girls or harem slaves hurrying home to escape a scolding.

When we came to the gates of the city, we were frightened lest we be stopped — but the Turkish soldiers guarding the gate had stolen for themselves some Armenian girls from refugees camped near the city, and were too busy amusing themselves with these girls to notice us. Soon we were beyond the city, alone in the night. The sands cut through our thin slippers, and we were afraid that every shadow was that of a lurking Kurd.

It was twenty miles or more, Arousiag believed, to the monastery. For three days we traveled, hiding most of the days in the sand for fear of wandering villagers or Kurds, and walking as far as we could at night. We had no bread or other food, and only late at night, when the dogs in the villages were asleep, could we dare to approach a village well for water.

Arousiag suffered much from thirst on the fourth day. She was so famished for water, of which we had none the night before, that when I cried she moistened her tongue with my tears. At last she could go no further and sank to the earth. In the distance was an Arab village. The Arabs are not like the Kurds — they are very fierce sometimes, and do not like the Armenians, but unless they are in the pay of Turkish pashas, they are not always cruel. To save Arousiag's life, I left her and went into the village.

The Arab women gathered around me, and to them I appealed for food and water, as best I could. The women pitied me, and when the Arab men came to inspect me, they, too, felt sorry. They brought a gourd of cool water, and bread, and some of the women went with me to where Arousiag lay. The water revived and strengthened her, and it gave me strength too. Our clothes were mostly torn away, and the Arab women gave us other garments and sandals for our feet. The monastery, they said, was but a few miles further on, and they showed us the nearest way. An Arab boy went with us to tell the men of other villages that we must not be harmed. Also the boy guided us away from a Circassian village, where we would have been made captives.

When the gray stone walls of the convent rose before us in the distance, Arousiag and I knelt down on the earth and thanked our Savior. The Arab boy turned and ran back when he saw we were praying to the Christ of the "unbelievers." But we were very grateful to him.

It was almost evening, and the monks were at prayer. We stood at the gate until some of them heard our call, and then they let us in. The monks were very kind. They gathered around us and listened to our story. Then they took us into their little chapel and knelt down around us, while the prior chanted a prayer of thankfulness. When the prayer was finished, a monk led us to a part of the monastery separated from the main buildings. Here we were astonished to find more than half a hundred Armenian girls and widowed brides, who, like us, had found refuge among the monks. Nearly all these girls and young women were from Van, the largest of the Armenian cities, or from districts nearby. Some were from Bitlis, where thousands of my people had been killed in a single hour, only the girls and brides being left alive for the pleasure of the Turks. Some had escaped from Diyarbekir.

All had been directed to the monastery as a refuge by friendly Arabs or Armenian Derders. One by one or in groups of two and three they had applied at the monastery gates just as had Arousiag and I, and the monks had taken them in, disregarding the great danger to themselves.

We all were cautioned not to show ourselves outside the smaller building which the monks had given over to us, lest wandering Kurds or soldiers chance to see us and thus discover that the monastery was the retreat of escaped refugees. The monks prayed with us twice every day and nursed back to health those who were ill. Little Arousiag became very glad when the prior assured her that God had understood, when she renounced Him, that in her heart she was still loyal to Him. When the aged prior knelt with her alone and prayed especially that God forgive her every blasphemous prayer she had made to Allah while under the eyes of the watchful harem women in the house of Hadji Ghafour, she was happy again.

For two weeks we were safe in the monastery. Then, suddenly, our peace was ended. One night, long after everyone in the monastery had gone to sleep, we were awakened by a great shouting and pounding at the gates. From our windows we could look into the yard, but we could not see the gate itself. While we huddled together in fright, we saw the little company of monks, hastily robed, led by their aged prior, carrying a lighted candle, move slowly across the yard. When they had passed out of our sight toward the gate, the shouting suddenly stopped, and we heard voices demanding that the gate be opened.

I think the monks refused. The shouting began again, and we saw the monks retreating across the yard. An instant later, a horde of strange figures, which we recognized as those of Tchetchens, or Circassian bandits, pushed across the yard to the monastery doors. When the monks refused to open the iron gates, they had climbed the walls.

Tchetchens are even more cruel and wicked than the Kurds. They are constantly at war, either with the Kurds and Arabs, or the Turks themselves. During the massacres, the Turks had propitiated them by giving them permission to prey upon the bands of Armenian exiles in their district and to steal as many Christian girls as they wished. Always in the past it has been the Tchetchens who have brought to the harems of the pashas their prettiest girls, as they do not hesitate to steal the daughters of their own people, the Circassians, for the slave markets of Constantinople and Smyrna.

The monks tried to barricade themselves in their chapel. The prior pleaded through the iron barred windows with the Tchetchen leader, appealing to him for the same consideration even the Kurds had always given the monastery. But the Tchetchen chief had learned in some manner that Armenian girls had been concealed in the monastery, and he demanded that we be surrendered as the price of mercy for the monks.

The monks refused to open their chapel doors or to reveal our hiding place. But the chapel doors were of wood — they gave way when the Tchetchens rushed against them. We heard the shrieks of our friends, the monks. There were cries for mercy, prayers to God and brutal shouts from the Tchetchens. In a little while there were no more screams, no more prayers — just the shouting of the bandits.

There was no escape for us. The Tchetchens were swarming about the yard below and through the chambers of the monastery proper. The only way out of the buildings the monks had set aside for us was through passages or windows leading directly into the yard. We heard one band of Tchetchens breaking in the door that opened into the rooms on the floor below us. We crowded into a corner and waited, trembling, too frightened even to pray.

The Tchetchens climbed the stone stairway. They were cursing their ill fortune at not having found us. One of them pushed in the door of the room in which we had gathered. The moon was shining through the windows and the bandits saw us. Then the spell of our silent fear was broken — we screamed. In an instant the Tchetchen band came pouring into the room.

They called terrible jests to each other. Arousiag and I were kneeling, with our arms around each other. A Tchetchen caught my hair in one hand and that of Arousiag in the other and dragged us down the stairway. The others were either dragged out in the same way or carried into the yard tossed across a Tchetchen's shoulder.

About the steps of the chapel we saw the bodies of the monks. All had been driven out of the chapel into the moonlight and then killed. The Tchetchens dragged us outside the monastery gate. They then gathered up their horses and drove them into the yard, where they could be left for the night. Then the Tchetchens returned to us.

Each claimed the girl or girls he had captured and dragged through the yard. Those who were not satisfied with their prizes, in comparing their beauty with those who had fallen to the lot of others, quarreled. Little Arousiag's arm was broken when one Tchetchen, seeing that the bandit who had captured us had two girls, pulled her away from him. Her captor paid no attention to her screams of pain. He subdued her by twisting her broken arm until she was unconscious.

When daylight came and the Tchetchens could see our faces more plainly, they selected those whom they considered the prettiest, and killed the rest. They killed Arousiag because of her broken arm. Then they lifted us onto their horses and took us to Diyarbekir.

X

THE GAME OF THE SWORDS, AND DIYARBEKIR

From the edge of a sandy plateau, I caught my first view of Diyarbekir, once the capital of our country. For two days we had ridden with the Tchetchens. We knew that some new peril awaited us in this ancient city which, centuries before, had been one of the most glorious cities of Christ.

When the Tchetchens drew up at the edge of the plateau, the walls of the city spread out far below us, with here and there a minaret rising over the low roofs. Just beyond the city was the beautiful, blue Tigris — the River Hiddekel, of the Bible. And as far as I could see, dotting the great plains that are watered by the Tigris, were Christian refugees from the north and east and west, thousands and thousands of them. Some had walked hundreds of miles. Nearly all the Armenians who were permitted to live that long were brought to Diyarbekir, where those who were not massacred in the city or outside the walls were turned south into the Syrian and Arabian deserts, to be deserted there.

More than one million of my people were started toward Diyarbekir when the deportations and massacres began. Only 100,000, I have heard, lived to reach the ancient city on the Tigris. And of these more than half were massacred within the city and outside the walls. Only young women and some of the children were saved, and these were lost in harems, or, as with the children, placed in Dervish monasteries to be taught Mohammedanism, so they might be sold as slaves when they grew up.

112

Nail Pasha, the Vali of Diyarbekir, was very wicked. Inside the city there are several ancient forts, built centuries ago — one of them in the days of Mohammed, and two great prisons. Already more than 3,000 Russian prisoners of war had been marched from the Caucasus to Diyarbekir for confinement in these prisons. Nail Pasha had taken away all the clothing of these prisoners, and had compelled them, by refusing to give them food, to work as masons on a large house the pasha was building for himself.

When the refugees began to arrive at Diyarbekir in great numbers, Nail Pasha crowded the Russians into one of the fortresses so closely they had almost no room to lie down at night. The other prisons he then filled with the Armenian men who had been permitted to accompany their women from some of the smaller Armenian villages in the north. When the prisons were full of these exiles, he had his soldiers massacre them. Outside the city their women waited on the plains or were taken away without even being told what had been the fate of their husbands, sons and brothers.

When more Russian prisoners arrived, Nail Pasha crowded Armenians into the prisons in the daytime and killed them, and then compelled the Russians to carry out the bodies and remove the blood before they could lie down to rest from their day's labor in the fields or on the stonework of his new house. The soldiers of Nail Pasha told with great enjoyment how the bodies of little Armenian children had been mixed in with cement and built into the walls of the new house to fill the spaces between the stones.

The Tchetchens who had stolen us from the monastery decided to enter the city by its southern gate — where the walls reach down almost to the river banks. But when they had galloped around that way, soldiers from the gate came out and told them the Vali had issued orders that no more refugees were to be brought into the city until some of those already within the walls were "cleared out" — massacred or sent away.

Afterward I learned why the city itself was crowded with refugees while so many others were camped outside the walls. The Vali promised protection from further deportation to all who had managed to preserve enough money to bribe him. These he allowed to go within the city and occupy deserted houses. When their money ran out the "protection" ceased, and they were sent out of the city in little companies — always to be killed at the gates by Tchetchens, who had been notified to wait for them.

When the Tchetchens saw they could not enter the city with us at once, they lifted us from their horses and ordered us to sit in a circle so they could guard us easily. Of the two hundred in the monastery, only twenty-seven of us still lived. Three of the girls were younger than I. None was more than twenty, although several had been brides when the massacres came.

The bandit leader then went into the city by himself. All that day, and the next, and most of the day after that, we sat in the sand in the burning sun. The Tchetchens foraged bread and berries and gave us just a little of what they did not want themselves. Only once each day would they let us have water. On the second day one of the girls became hot with fever. She cried for water, and when a Tchetchen would have slapped her for her cries, she showed him her tongue, which had begun to swell. When the Tchetchen saw this, he called to his comrades, and they were afraid lest the fever spread to others of us. They paid no attention to the poor girl's pleading for water, but dragged her a hundred feet away and left her. Once she got to her feet and seemed to be trying to get back to us. A Tchetchen went out to her and struck her down with the end of his gun. She could not get up again, and we saw her rolling about in the sand until she died.

On the evening of our second day of waiting outside the walls, there was a great commotion at the city's southern gate, and presently a stream of refugees, all women, came pouring out onto the plain. All that day groups of Tchetchen horsemen had been gathering from the surrounding country and taking up positions nearby. Now we knew why these horsemen had come — they had been notified a company of refugees was to be sent out of the city.

The Turks themselves seldom massacred women in a wholesale way. Constantinople had not authorized the killing of submissive women — the work was left to Kurds and other bands.

I think there must have been more than 2,000 women and some children in this company. They began to come out of the gate before sundown, and were still coming long after it was dark. The Tchetchens herded them into a circle about one mile from the walls. They were half a mile or more from us, but when the moon came up, we could plainly hear the shouts and screams that told us the Tchetchens had begun their evil work.

All night long we heard the screams. Sometimes they would be very near, as if fugitives were coming our way. Then we would hear shouts and the hoofbeats of horses. There would be piercing shrieks and then only the sound of hoofbeats growing fainter. The Tchetchens who guarded us did not bother us, they seemed to be saving us for something else. But we could not sleep that night. Sometimes even now I cannot sleep, although I am safe forever. Those screams come to me in the night time, and even with my friends all about me, I cannot shut them out of my ears.

When the first gray mist of dawn spread over the plain, the excitement was still at its height. Then, suddenly, everything was quiet. We were too far from the city to hear the voices on the minarets, but we knew that silence meant that the hour for the Prayer of Islam had arrived. Even in the midst of their awful work, the Tchetchens instinctively heard the call and stopped to kneel toward Mecca. I remember how I wondered that morning, while the bandits were reciting their prayer to their Allah for his grace and commendation, how my Christ would feel if His people should come to Him in prayer at the sunrise after such a night's work as that.

More than ever before I loved Jesus Christ and trusted Him that morning while the Mohammedan bandits were praying to him they call Allah.

I think less than 300 of that company of Armenians were alive when the sun came up and we could see across the plain. One little group we saw moving about, huddled together. All around them were the Tchetchens searching the bodies scattered over a great circle — making sure in the daylight they had missed nothing of value in the massacre and robbery during the night.

During the morning the Tchetchens busied themselves with the young women who had been permitted to survive the night. We could see them go up to the little group of survivors and drag some of them away.

It was when the Tchetchens began to tire of this that we saw them preparing, a little way from where we were, in a flat place on the plain, for one of the pastimes for which wild Circassian tribes are famous, and which they frequently repeated, as I afterward learned, as long as my people lasted.

They planted their swords, which were the long, slender-bladed swords that came from Germany, in a long row in the sand, so the sharp pointed blades rose out of the ground as high as would be a very small child. When we saw these preparations, all of us knew what was going to happen. When Armenian children are bad, their mothers sometimes tell them the Tchetchens will come and get them if they don't be good. And when the children ask, "And when the Tchetchens come, what will they do?" their mothers say:

"The Tchetchens are very wicked robber horsemen, who like to sharpen their swords with little boys and girls."

Already I was trembling with sickness of heart because of the awful night before and the things I had seen that morning when daylight came. The other women beside me were trembling, too, and felt as if they would rather die than see any more. We begged our Tchetchens to take us away — to take us where we could not look upon those sword blades — but they only laughed at us and told us we must watch and be thankful to them we were under their protection.

When the long row of swords had been placed, the Tchetchens hurried back to the little band of Armenians. We saw them crowd among them, and then come away carrying, or dragging, all the young women who were left — maybe fifteen or twenty — I could not count them.

Each girl was forced to stand with a dismounted Tchetchen holding her on her feet, half way between two swords in the long row. The captives cried and begged, but the cruel bandits were heedless of their pleadings.

When the girls had been placed to please them, one between each two sword blades, the remaining Tchetchens mounted their horses and gathered at the end of the line. At a shouted signal, the first one galloped down the row of swords. He seized a girl, lifted her high in the air and flung her down upon a sword point, without slackening his horse. It was a game — a contest!

Each Tchetchen tried to seize as many girls as he could and fling them upon the sword points, so that they were killed in the one throw, in one gallop along the line. Only the most skillful of them succeeded in impaling more than one girl. Some lifted the second from the ground, but missed the sword in their speed, and the girl, with broken bones or bleeding wounds, was held up in the line again to be used in the "game" a second time — praying that this time the Tchetchen's aim would be true and the sword put an end to her torture.

In the meantime the Jews of Diyarbekir had come out from the city, driven by gendarmes, to gather up the bodies of the slain Armenians. They brought carts and donkeys with bags swung across their backs. Into the carts and bags, they piled the corpses and took them to the banks of the Tigris, where the Turks made them throw their burdens into the water. This is one of the persecutions the Jews were forced to bear. The Mohammedans did not kill them, but they liked to compel them to do such awful tasks.

Late in the afternoon, the chief of our Tchetchens came out from the city. His men drew off to one side and talked with him excitedly. When it grew dark, they lifted us upon their horses and carried us into the city through the south gate. At the gate, the Tchetchen chief showed to the officers of the gendarmes a paper he had brought from the city, and the Tchetchens were permitted to enter. We passed through dark narrow streets until we came to a house terraced high above the others, with an iron gate leading into a courtyard off the street. A hammal, or Turkish porter, was waiting at the gate and swung it open.

The bandits dismounted outside the gate to the house and lifted us to the ground. The leader waved us inside. With half a dozen of his men he entered behind us and the gate closed. Some of the Tchetchens went into the house. In a few minutes they came out, followed by a foreign man, whose uniform I recognized as that of a German soldier.

Servants followed with lighted lamps, and the soldier looked into our faces and examined us shamefully. Only eight of the girls pleased him. I was among these. We were pushed into the house and the door was closed behind us. Then we heard the Tchetchens gather up the other girls and take them into the street. I do not know what became of them. The soldier and the servants, all of whom were foreigners, whom I afterward discovered were Germans, took us into a stone floored room which had been used as a stable for horses.

It must have been two or three hours afterward — after midnight, I think; we could not keep track of the time — when the soldier and the servants came for us. Before they took us from the stable room, they took away what few clothes we had. They led us, afraid and ashamed, into a room where were three men in the uniforms of German officers. The soldiers saluted them. The officers seemed very pleased when they had looked at us. We tried to cover ourselves with our arms and to hide behind each other, but the soldier roughly drew us apart. The officers laughed at our embarrassment, and then dismissed the soldier, saying something to him in German, which I do not understand.

The officers talked among themselves, also in German. They tried to caress us. It amused them greatly when we pleaded with them to spare us, to let us have clothes and to have mercy, in God's name.

Almost two weeks I was a prisoner in this house. The principal officer's name was Captain August Walsenburg. He was middle-aged, I think, and very bald. After a while I learned many things about him. He had been connected with a German trading company, the "Oriental Handelsgesellschaft," in the city of Van.

He was a reserve army officer and had been called into service. He helped the Turkish officials at Van mobilize an army there and had taken part in the Armenian massacres at that city. He had been ordered to report to a German general whose name I do not remember at Aleppo, where the German commander was organizing Turkish soldiers for the Mesopotamian armies. But when he reached Diyarbekir, there was news of the Russian advance in the Caucasus, and he had been ordered, by telegraph, to wait at Diyarbekir for instructions. The two other officers were lieutenants, who had accompanied him from Van, and they, too, were awaiting instructions.

They were the only German officers at Diyarbekir at that time. The Vali was very friendly with them. He had set aside for them the house to which we were taken as captives. To this house were brought many pretty Armenian girls stolen by the Kurds and Tchetchens. When they tired of them, they sent them away to the refugee camps outside the city or to be sold to Turks.

The German captain asked me to be submissive. I fought him with all my might. I told him he might kill me. This amused him. It was while I was his prisoner I tasted, for the first and only time in my life that which I have learned in America is called "whiskey". It was bitter and terrible. The officers had brought some of this from Van. They drank much of it, and it made them very brutal. One night they assembled all the girls in the house into a room where they were eating and forced them to sit on a table and drink this awful whiskey. They were delighted when it made us ill.

One by one the other girls who had been stolen with me from the monastery were sent away, after the officers had wearied of them, and their places were taken by new ones. I think I was kept because I fought so hard when one of them approached me. The captain always clapped his hands and laughed aloud when I fought.

There was another girl, who had been a prisoner in the house longer than others — since before I was taken there. She had especially pleased one of the under-officers. She told me of one night when the officers had taken much of their whiskey and were particularly cruel. She said they sent for some of the girls then in the house and, standing them sideways, shot at them with their pistols, using their breasts as targets. Afterward I was told this thing was done very often by the Turks in the Vilayet of Van when they massacred our people there.

At last orders came to the officers to leave Diyarbekir. I understood they would have to go to Harpout. They prepared to leave immediately and set out the next morning. They had in the house many rugs and articles of valuable jewelry they had bought from Kurds and Tchetchens, who had stolen them from Armenians, and all of this booty they carefully packed in boxes to be kept for them by the Vali until a caravan bound for the railway at Ras-el-Ain came through.

They were so hurried they paid little attention to us. When they left all their servants accompanied them, riding donkeys behind their masters' horses. So we were alone in the house.

We would have been happy in our deliverance had it not been for the danger which threatened us at the hands of the Turkish gendarmes, who would be sure to discover us. We searched until we found where the servants had hidden our clothes in a dark room, into which the clothes of all Armenian girls who had been brought to the house had been thrown. We each took something with which to cover ourselves.

We spent a day and night in constant terror of discovery. We were afraid to venture into the streets and afraid to stay where we were. There were many foreign missionaries in the city, including Americans, but they lodged in a different quarter, and we never could have reached them. The gendarmes came the third day after the officers left. I do not think they expected to find anyone in the house, but came to look for things the Germans might have left unpacked.

We saw them entering through the courtyard gate. There was no place we could hide, as the house was built in tiers. We could only huddle in a corner and put off our capture till the last minute. The gendarmes saw us from the courtyard and rushed after us with shouts.

When I ran through the room that had been occupied by one of the officers, I saw a knife he had left behind. I seized this and hid it in my clothes. It was the first time I had held a knife in my hands or other weapon since I was taken from my home in Tchemesh-Gedzak.

A gendarme cornered me in one of the rooms, just as all the other girls were trapped. He caught me by the arms. He was taking me into another room when the officer of the gendarmes saw me. He halted the man, took me from him and ordered him to "find another one for himself." The officer pushed me into the room.

But when he tried to pinion my arms, I turned on him with the knife.

I know God guided my hand, for I am sure I killed him. He fell at my feet.

In other parts of the house and in the courtyard the gendarmes were giving their attention to the girls they had found. I reached the street without being seen. I looked in each direction and could see no one except a Turkish woman, who came out of her gate on the opposite side of the street. For an instant I thought I would be caught, and I gripped the knife, which I still kept under my clothes.

But the Turkish woman was kind. She pitied me. She stepped back into her gate and motioned me to follow. I was afraid, yet I trusted her. She closed the gate and took me in her arms. She was sorry for me and my people, she said, and would help me. But she dared not take me into her house. She told me I could hide in her yard till night, when I might slip out of the city to where the refugees were.

During the day she brought me food. At dark she came to take leave of me, and kissed me, and gave me three liras, which was all she could spare without earning a scolding from her husband. "Go out by the north gate, not by the south gate," she said to me. "All the refugees who are taken around by the south gate are killed; those who are camped beyond the north gate may live. But do not join them while it still is night, or you may be caught in a massacre. Hide among the rocks in the pass through the Kara-jah hills, a mile from the city. If the Armenians are allowed to pass these rocks when they are taken away, it means they will be allowed to live through another stage of their journey."

I reached the gate without being stopped, as I was careful to keep in the shadows. Gendarmes guarded the gate, but they were not very watchful. I ran onto the plain and followed the directions the friendly Turkish lady had given me until I came to the rocks which marked the road through the low hills that skirted the city on the north. Along this road the refugees sent to the southern deserts from Diyarbekir must pass.

I waited at the rocks through the night. In the morning I thought to walk along the road to where I would not be seen by soldiers, Kurds or Tchetchens roving on the plains near the city, and where I could wait until a company of my people passed.

But while I was picking my way through the narrow pass between the rocks, I saw a little group of zaptiehs coming toward me along the road beyond. I had not expected to meet any one. I screamed before I could stop myself. The zaptiehs heard me and I ran back into the shelter of the rocks and drew out my knife, which I had kept so I might kill myself rather than be stolen again. But I was afraid God would not approve. While the zaptiehs searched the rocks, I knelt in a crevice and asked God to tell me what I should do — if He would blame me if I killed myself before the zaptiehs found me. "Dear God, tell me, shall I come now to You or wait until You call?" I asked of Him.

I know He heard me, and I know He answered. For something told me to throw the knife far away — and I did.

That was God's will, I know, for after a while He was to lead me into the arms of my mother that I might be with her once again before the Turks killed her.

XI

"ISHIM YOK; KEIFIM TCHOK!"

I threw the knife away and stood up. The zaptiehs soon found me. I was resigned for whatever was to happen, and did not run from them.

I told them I had come out from the city; that I wanted to join some of my people; that if they would not harm me, I would not give them any trouble. I still had the three liras, or three pounds, which the good Turkish lady had given me, but I knew if I gave it to them, they would only search me for more and then, perhaps, kill me. So I told them I would get money for them from my people if they would let me join a company that was not to be killed.

"Maybe all will be killed; maybe not all. We do not know. Come with us. Get us money and we will let you live," one of them said to me.

I walked with them a little way, until we saw coming toward us a long line of refugees. Then the zaptiehs halted, and from what they said to each other, I knew they had been sent from a village a little way behind us to join the guards escorting this party.

Soon the party drew near. The zaptiehs said I must stay near the front of the line, and that they would come after a while and hunt for me, and that I must have money or they would take me off and kill me. They came to me a few hours later, and I gave them the three liras, and they kept their promise and did not molest me again.

The party of refugees I had joined was from Erzeroum and the little cities in that district. My heart leaped with joy when I saw among them a few Armenian men. It was the first time I had seen

123

men of my people for so long, and I was so happy for the women whose husbands and fathers could still be with them. When I was led up to this party by the zaptiehs, the first women to see me held out their arms to me. They thought I was one of the girls of their own party who had been stolen the night before. When I told them I had escaped from Diyarbekir, they were glad for me, and one lady who had lost her sixteen-year-old daughter to the Turks said I might take this daughter's place and march with her. Another little daughter, six years old, was with her still.

There were two thousand, or a few more, in this party. They were all that were left of 40,000 Armenian families who had been deported from Erzeroum and nearby villages. Erzeroum is 150 miles directly north of Diyarbekir, but the Armenians there had been sent to Diyarbekir in two directions. Some had come by way of Erzindjan and Malatia. These had walked almost 300 miles.

DRIVEN FORTH ON THE ROAD OF TERROR
The old and the very young just leaving their home in an ancient city, on their way to the desert. In the foreground is a zaptieh, who has stolen an armful of rugs from the exiles.

Others had come by way of Khnuss and Bitlis, and these had walked 250 miles. The survivors of both parties reached Diyarbekir at almost the same time as those who came by way of Bitlis had been kept for many days at towns along the route.

The only friend the Armenians at Erzeroum had when they were being assembled for deportation was the good Badvelli, Robert Stapleton, the American vice-consul, whose home is in New York City. Dr. Stapleton took all the Armenian girls he could crowd into his house at Erzeroum, and when the Turks came for them, he showed the Turks the American flag over his door, and ordered them away. There were many mothers in this party when I joined it who were glad their daughters had been among those who were left under Dr. Stapleton's protection, and they wondered if they still were safe.

Many months later I learned the good American Badvelli kept them all safely until the Russians came to Erzeroum and took them under their care.

There were almost 75,000 men, women and children in the parties that went by way of Erzindjan. Of these only 500 reached Diyarbekir. All the prettiest and youngest girls had been stolen by the Kurds or zaptiehs and given to Turks along the way. The girl children under ten years old had all been either killed, if they were not strong and pretty, or sold to the Turks, who kept them to raise as Moslems for their harems or sent them to Constantinople to be sold into the harems of wealthy Turks there. Many of the younger women who were not stolen had been outraged to death. All the grandmothers and women who were ill had been abandoned at the roadside, or killed outright. So only the 500 remained.

Of the other parties, which had numbered 50,000 individuals, and who had mostly come from the smaller cities near Erzeroum, with many rich families, including teachers, bankers, merchants and professional men from the city itself, among them, only 1,500 were left — about 300 men, I think.

When the different parties recognized each other in camp outside Diyarbekir, they rejoiced greatly, and they were allowed to move their camps together. They remained outside Diyarbekir eleven days, because all of them had been robbed of their money and all valuables, so they could not bribe the Vali to let them stay inside the city.

Each night while they were camped outside Diyarbekir, Turks came forth from the city to steal girls, and soldiers came out to borrow girls and young women for a little while. They had no food except one loaf of bread for each person, every other day, sent out by the Vali, and occasionally something which American missionaries in the city managed to smuggle out to them by bribing Turkish water carriers.

During the night, while I was hiding in the rocks, they were told they were to be taken away again in the morning, this time to Ourfa. They had begged the Turkish officers to let them stay a while longer, because so many of them were suffering with swollen feet, which had grown more painful, even to bursting, during their eleven days of rest. They asked to be allowed to wait until their feet were better again, but the Turks would not grant this.

So they had started early in the morning, and now I was with them, and before me lay the long walk to Ourfa, 200 miles further toward the Arabian deserts — unless I suffered the harder fate of being stolen again along the way.

For the first time since I had been taken from my home that Easter Sunday morning, so many weeks before, I learned, when I joined this party on the way to Ourfa, where my people were being taken — those who were allowed to live. Soldiers who went out to the refugee camps from Diyarbekir had told these exiles that all who reached Aleppo, a large city on the Damascus railway, were to be taken from there to the Der-el-Zor district, on the southern Euphrates, and there put to building military roads through the deserts. As only a few men lived to reach there, the strong women were to be used.

But always there was hope of deliverance. So many Armenians had friends in America, sons and brothers who had left our country to go to the wonderful United States. They prayed every night that from America would come help before all were dead. There were rumors even then that help was coming; that good people in the United States were sending money and food and clothing and trying to get the Turks to be more merciful. It was this hope that kept thousands alive.

When I joined this party it could only move along very slowly, because of swollen feet. When we came to the rocks where I had been discovered it was very painful for those whose feet were

126

broken open to pass between them, because the pass was very narrow and the stones sharp. For more than a mile we had to walk along this rocky defile — then we came into the open again. I had a pair of sandals, with leather bottoms, which I had saved from the house of the Germans. These I gave to the lady who had asked me to march with her, for her own feet were bleeding. No one else in the party had shoes or slippers or any covering for their feet, except rags which some could spare from their clothing.

Outside Diyarbekir some of the refugees had traded laces which they had saved by wrapping them around their bodies, for donkeys and arabas (ox carts). They had been told they might keep these until they reached Ourfa. In the arabas they had hidden many small pieces of bread which they had saved from their occasional rations at Diyarbekir, hoping thus to provide against the sufferings of starvation along the road. But when they reached the rocks the pass was so narrow there was great trouble getting the arabas through.

Some Turkish villagers from the other side had come to the rocks, and when they saw the trouble the refugees were having with their arabas, they asked the zaptiehs guarding us why they could not have the donkeys and the carts. The zaptiehs told them if they would give some money to be divided among the guards, they could take them.

So the villagers paid money to the zaptiehs and then swooped down upon us and took away our animals and carts. They would not allow us to take what few belongings were in the carts, and the pieces of bread, saying they had bought everything the carts contained from the zaptiehs.

In one of the carts were two little girl twins, nine years old, whose mother had died at Diyarbekir. They were being taken care of by their aunt, who had three times bribed soldiers to let them alone, until she had nothing more to bribe with. She had hidden them in her araba, thinking she could save them and spare them the weary walking. The villager who took her cart refused to let her take them out. He said they went with the cart.

The woman was crazed, and screamed loudly. She attacked the villager with her hands. An Armenian man was near, and he and many women rushed at the Turk, who was alone. Three zaptiehs rushed up, but the women and the man were determined, and the zaptiehs were afraid to help the villager. They told him to let the aunt have the two little girls.

Although there were about 2,000 refugees in this party, I could count only eleven zaptiehs sent along as guards. As many men as could be spared by the Turks at Diyarbekir had been sent north to the army, and the supply of guards for refugees was very short. Had there been more zaptiehs they would not have hindered the Turk from stealing the little girls.

At the next village the zaptiehs decided they would have to have more help if they were to enjoy the license customary among them along the road. At this village they stopped us and held a long conversation with the Mudir, or village chief. Soon after the Mudir approached, followed by twenty or thirty of the most evil looking Turks I ever saw. Each one of them carried a gun and wore on his sleeve a strip of red woolen cloth, the badge of police authority.

When we went on these Turks were distributed among us by the zaptiehs as additional guards.

During the second day, upon the road we met a party of mounted Turkish soldiers, escorting a group of very comfortable looking covered arabas, such as are used by the wealthy for traveling in the interior of Turkey. In these arabas there were forty hanums, or Turkish wives, who were on their way with the soldier escort to Erzeroum, to join their husbands, who were high military officers with the army in the great military fortress there. They had come from Damascus, Beirut and Aleppo.

When our party approached, the arabas of the hanums halted, and the soldiers ordered our guards to halt us also. Then we saw that several of the arabas were occupied by young Armenian girls, from eight to twelve years old, all very sweet and gentle looking, as if they were the daughters of wealthy families. Some of them waved their little hands from under the curtains, and that is how we discovered them. From six to ten were crowded in each of their arabas, and each of the hanum's arabas hid others.

The little girls told us they were from Ourfa and Aleppo. Their parents and relatives all had been killed, and they had been given to the hanums, who, they understood, intended to put a part of them in Moslem schools at Erzeroum, so they could have them for sale when they were a little older. The others the hanums would keep as servants or to sell at once to friends among rich Turks.

The hanums descended from their arabas and asked our zaptiehs if there were any very pretty girl children among us. The zaptiehs did not approve of losing girl children to these Turkish wives, who, they thought, would take them without paying for them. So they said there were none. But one of the hanums saw a little girl holding onto her mother, and insisted upon having her brought to her. When she looked at the little girl closely, she saw she was pretty, and commanded one of the soldiers to take her into her carriage.

The child's mother held onto it desperately, and when the hanum, with her soldier near, put her hands on the little girl to pull it away the mother lost her reason and struck at her.

The soldier immediately caught hold of the woman and asked of the hanum, "What shall I do with her?" The hanum said, "Have we any oil to burn her?" The soldier said, "I do not think so." Then the hanum held out her hand and the soldier gave her his pistol. The Turkish woman went up to the mother and shot her with her own hands. She then caught the little girl's hand and led her to the araba. The little one wanted to kiss her mother, but the hanum jerked her away.

With our party was the wife of Abouhayatian Agha, the great scholar, of Van, who had escaped, when the massacres began, to Diyarbekir. Her husband had been a friend of Djevdet Bey. When the soldiers were turned loose upon the Armenians at Van, so Mrs. Abouhayatian told me, her husband went to Djevdet Bey and remonstrated with him. His reply, now famous all over Turkey, was: "Ishim yok; keifim tchok," which means, "I have no work to do; I have much fun!" After that, whenever regular soldiers were sent to slaughter Armenians, they called out to each other:

"Ishim yok; keifim tchok!"

Over this same path I walked, more than 400,000 of my people had trod — some of them having walked a thousand miles or more to get there. And of these, sole survivors of the millions who were deported from their homes, those who are alive today are lost in the deserts, where there is no bread or food.

God grant that I may soon go back to this desert, from which I escaped, with money and food for those of my people who may still be alive!

When we camped near a village at night, our zaptiehs would invite the village gendarme and his friends to come out, and they would sell young women to them for the night. The mother or other relatives of these young women dared not even object, for if they did the zaptiehs would kill them. Sometimes there would be better class Turks in some of these villages, and they would pick out girl children and buy them. They would pay our guards for the child they fancied and take it out of its mother's arms. These children now are being taught to be Moslems, and, if they are old enough, made to work in the fields. Some of them are concubines besides.

Three babies were born during the first days of this journey. The mothers were not allowed to rest along the way, neither before nor after. They were made to keep up with the party until the little ones were born. Sometimes the men would carry the mother a little way, but when the zaptiehs saw them doing this they would make them put her down. They would say the woman didn't deserve to be carried because she was bringing an unbeliever into the world.

These events always amused the zaptiehs greatly. When one of them discovered a baby was about to be born, he would call his comrades, and they would walk near the poor woman, making her keep on her feet until the last minute. Then they would stand close to her and laugh and jest. As soon as the baby was born, the mother would have to get upon her feet and walk. If she could not walk, the zaptiehs would leave her on the road and make the party move on.

Almost always the zaptiehs killed the babies. The first two born near me they took from the mothers and threw up in the air and caught them like a ball. They did this four or five times and then threw them away. The mothers saw, but they had to walk on. The third baby was not killed. He was born in the evening, just after we had camped. The zaptiehs were busy with their horses and did not notice. This one was a sweet little boy. Its father was dead. Its mother was so happy — and so sad, both together — when she first held it in her arms. She asked God to let it live, but there was no way. She had had so little food herself she could not nurse it. The little thing starved to death in her arms.

When we left the district where the villages were, we began to suffer for water. The zaptiehs carried great water bags over their saddles, but they would give none of it to us. For days at a time we marched without a drop of moisture to quench our thirst. Then we would come to a group of houses where Turks lived around a well, or spring. The Turks always would refuse to let us go near the wells, demanding pay for each gourd of water. Men would stand guard at the wells with guns and sticks to drive us off if we went near.

But no one in our party had anything left to pay with. Our women would go as near to the houses as they dared, and get down on their knees and beg for just a swallow of the precious water. Sometimes the Turks would let us go to the wells when they were convinced we had nothing to give them. But not always. At one place the head man, who had been a pilgrim and was called Hadji, demanded that if we could not give him money or rugs, we must give him for the community three strong men who could help till the fields which were watered from his spring.

We appealed to our guards, but they would not take our part. They stood by the Turks, and said if we wanted water, we should be willing to pay. At least thirty of our party had died that day for want of drink. Some of the women's tongues were so swollen they could not talk. There was talk of rushing on the spring in a body, but we knew this would cost many lives, for our zaptiehs stood near with their guns, and we knew, too, it would be held against us and probably cause a massacre.

Finally, Harutoune Yegarian, who had been a student at Erzeroum, said he would sacrifice himself. He asked if there were two other men who would give themselves. Two men whose wives had died, and who had no daughters, at once said they were willing. Many women embraced them. Harutoune was standing near me, and I cried for him. He saw me.

"Don't weep for me, little girl," he said to me.

131

"Every Armenian in the world should be glad to give himself for his people." Then he kissed me, and I think his kiss was the kiss of God.

The three men said they would stay and work in the field for the Turks, and so they let us have water — all we could drink and carry away.

When we reached the city of Severeg, half way to Ourfa, we had not had water for four days. There are three open wells on one side of Severeg, and they feed an artificial lake, which was filled when we arrived.

Some of our women were so parched they threw themselves into the lake and were drowned. Others could not wait until they reached the lake, and jumped into the wells.

So many did this they choked the wells, and the Turks, who had come out to meet us, had to pull them out. We who had kept our senses crowded around those who were pulled out and moistened our tongues from their wet clothes. After we left Severeg a fever attacked our party. Every day many died by the wayside. The zaptiehs rode at a distance away from us, and when any of the men or women dropped behind, they would shoot them. The fever parched the throats of those who suffered from it so badly that when we came to the next group of houses where there was a well the men braved the guns of the Turks and zaptiehs and rushed up to them.

After that the zaptiehs were wary of persecuting us too much, but we paid the penalty at Sheitan Deressi, or "Devil's Gorge," which we reached on the twenty-third day out of Diyarbekir.

When all our party had entered the gorge the zaptiehs left their horses and climbed above us and opened fire upon us. We were trapped so we could not turn back and could not escape. The zaptiehs picked off all the men. From early morning until dark, they continued shooting from the walls of the gorge, and at each shot a man fell. When evening came, all had been killed or mortally wounded.

When night fell the zaptiehs came down and began killing women with their knives and bayonets. They picked out the older women first, and soon all these were dead. When the moon lighted up the gorge the zaptiehs picked out the young married women — or those who had been married but now were widows — and amused themselves by mutilating them. They would not kill them outright, but would cut off their fingers, or their hands, or their breasts. They tore out the eyes of some. When dawn came, only those who had succeeded in hiding behind rocks, or we who were young and might be sold to Turks, were alive. During the next day I counted, and there were only 160 left of the 2,000 who left Diyarbekir with me. I have heard it said that more than 300,000 of my people were killed in this spot during the period of the massacres.

Now that we were so few, the zaptiehs made us march faster, and as we were nearly all young, they were more cruel to us. I was glad that morning when I discovered that the lady who had let me march with her had survived. She had hidden during the night, and had saved her little girl too. But my gladness for her soon became sorrow. The little girl was taken with the fever that day. The next day she could not walk any more. When the zaptiehs discovered she was suffering from the fever, they commanded the mother to leave her at the roadside. The mother laid the little girl down, but she could not leave her when the child held out her arms and cried. A zaptieh came up with his bayonet pointed, ready to kill the mother, and I pulled her away and comforted her. Every step or two the mother would look back until we could not see her little girl any more.

XII

REUNION — AND THEN, THE SHEIKH ZILAN

WITH so few of us to guard, and almost all of us either young or not so very old, the nights were made terrible by the zaptiehs. For many days they had been on the road with us, and had tired of ordinary cruelties and the mere shaming of the girls under cover of darkness at the camping places. The Turks who had been recruited from the villages and made guards over us were especially brutal. It was their first opportunity to visit upon Christians that hatred with which Islam looks upon the "Unbeliever."

When we drew near to Ourfa we were joined by a party numbering, I think, four or five hundred exiles from the Sandjak of Marash, a subdistrict north of the Amanus, of which Zeitoun, Albustan and Marash are the large cities. Nearly all of these were from the city of Marash itself — some from Zeitoun. The removal of the Armenians from the Sandjak of Marash was begun later than in other parts of Asia Minor. When Haidar Pasha first issued the orders for deportation some of the Armenians who had arms resisted. They refused to leave or submit to the zaptiehs unless they were given guarantees they would be allowed to return to their homes after the war.

Haidar Pasha had few soldiers at his command just then. He sent to Aleppo for assistance to carry out his wish to send the Armenians away. From Aleppo came Captain Schappen, a German artillery officer, who was stationed there with other German officers. Captain Schappen organized large bodies of zaptiehs and taught them the use of machine guns. He then led them personally,

134

and with other German officers and their aides made a raid on the Armenian houses. In quarters where there was resistance, he turned the machine guns on the houses.

From Marash and nearby cities, fourteen thousands of my people, men, women and children, were sent away, guarded by the zaptiehs, under the command of this captain. For some reason which none of the Christians knew, these exiles were not taken directly into the desert toward Bagdad, as were others from that district, but they were kept many days, even weeks at a time, in camp with almost no food or water, then to move on only a few miles and to camp again. They were many weeks reaching the vicinity of Ourfa. When they joined us, of the fourteen thousand who were torn from their homes only the three or four hundred remained alive! No men were left — just mothers and daughters and aunts and nieces.

Captain Schappen had returned, after three weeks on the road, to Aleppo. He took with him a Miss Tchilingarian, who was fifteen years old, and who had just returned from a private school in Germany, where her parents had sent her to be educated. She was home on a vacation when the deportation began. She was very pretty, those who knew her told me, and had already won honors in music. Her family intended she should become a singer and take to the Christian world outside Turkey the beautiful folk ballads of my people. Captain Schappen marked her during the first night on the road, and had her taken to his tent. He then designated a zaptieh to be her especial guard until he took her away with him. He also took with him Mrs. Sarafian, the young wife of Dr. Dikran Sarafian, who had been educated in Switzerland, and was one of the most prominent Armenian physicians in central Turkey. Mrs. Sarafian was a Swiss, and had learned to love Dr. Sarafian while he was a student in her country. She had come to Marash to marry him just two years before. Captain Schappen had her taken to his tent also, soon after they began their march, and when her husband objected, the officer ordered a zaptieh to shoot him.

When Captain Schappen and his companions decided to return to Aleppo, they sent zaptiehs scouring the country for miles around looking for donkeys. For these, the officers traded girl children. A pretty child was given for one donkey. Of the children who were plain the officers gave two, or sometimes three, for a single donkey. Thus they collected a large herd of donkeys, which probably were needed by the army.

In another day after this remnant of the Christians of Marash joined us, we came into sight of Ourfa. We were ordered to camp close to an artificial lake — such a lake as often is found outside Moslem cities. The leaders of our zaptiehs rode into the city for instructions. Soon Turks, in long white coats, came out of the city to look at us. When they saw that ours was a party of almost all younger women, with girl children still left, they spread the news in Ourfa, and in a little while dozens of Turks came out in little groups of four and five.

They tried to persuade our zaptiehs to let them carry away with them the young women and children they wanted. The zaptiehs would not permit this, however, unless they were paid what was then considered high prices for Christian women. They said they had brought us this far, and now they intended to profit — that they had only permitted us to live because they hoped to get "good prices" for the choicest of us in the Ourfa market.

The Turks did not want to pay the high prices, and the zaptiehs would not trade with them. The zaptiehs said there was a good market in Ourfa for pretty Armenian women, and they preferred to get the Mutassarif's permission to hunt purchasers there who would bid against each other. The Turks went back to the city disappointed.

That night, just after sundown, these same Turks came out again and opened the sluices that held the artificial lake, allowing the water to spread over the plain and flood our camp. We had to run as fast as we could to scramble to safety, and there was great confusion. Even the zaptiehs were caught by surprise.

In this confusion the Turks rushed in among us and helped themselves to our youngest girls — the prettiest children they could seize. We were powerless to save them, as each of the Turks carried a heavy stick, with which they beat down the mothers or relatives who tried to rescue their little ones. By the time we had escaped the water and assembled again, and the zaptiehs were recovered from their own panic, the Turks were gone — and with them fifteen or twenty beautiful little girls.

Later I learned what was the immediate fate of the children stolen when the lake was opened on us. Haidar Pasha had seized the ancient Catholic Armenian monastery there, and had transformed it into a "government school for refugee children." Since I have come to America, I have learned that when complaints were made to the Sultan at Constantinople by foreign ambassadors of the stealing of children, the Sultan's officials replied that they were taken as a kindly deed by the government, which wished to place them in comfort in the "government school" at Ourfa and other cities.

But this is what the "government school" at Ourfa was:

Haidar Pasha sent his soldiers, under command of a bey, to take possession of the monastery, a large stone building. They surrounded it and forced the monks, among them Father Antone and Father Shiradjian, two priests who were much beloved by Protestant as well as Catholic Armenians, to walk in between two rows of soldiers. The soldiers closed in behind them and marched with them outside the walls of the city. Then the soldiers halted and the Bey asked how many there were among the monks who were willing to take the oath of Islam and forswear Christ.

When the Bey ceased speaking, Father Antone lifted his voice with the words of an ancient song of the good Saint Thomas Aquinas, and all the monks joined in. While they sang the soldiers shot them down — volley after volley — until all were dead. The last monk to fall died with the words of the song on his lips.

Haidar Pasha then cleared out the monastery of all its relics and religious symbols. Among these were some things which were very dear to my people. There was, for instance, a piece of the lance which pierced the side of Jesus at the Crucifixion. What has become of this and other things that were associated with Christ, Himself, and kept by the Fathers in this monastery I do not know. It is said they were taken to Damascus and placed in a mosque there, to be ridiculed by the Moslems.

When the monastery was cleared, Haidar Pasha gathered from among the Armenians who were then being taken out of the city, a number of Armenian girls of the best families and confined them in the monastery. He then seized hundreds of Armenian girl children, from 7 to 12 years old, and shut them in the monastery, to be taught the Moslem religion and raised as Moslems. He compelled the older girls to teach them the beliefs of Islam, under penalty of the most awful cruelties. To this monastery then came rich Turks from all over Asia Minor to select as many little girls as they wished and could buy for their harems — where they would grow up to be submissive slaves.

While we were waiting outside the city for the zaptiehs to dispose of us according to whatever their plans might be, I saw coming toward us, out of a city gate, a company of hamidieh, or Kurd cavalry, with a supply train of donkeys and arabas, which indicated a long journey ahead. There must have been a full regiment of the horsemen, as they filled the plain outside the city while forming their line of march.

When they drew near, to pass us within a hundred yards or so, I saw a little group of women and children riding on donkeys and ponies between the lines of horsemen. I recognized these as Armenians. This was an unusual sight — Armenians under protection instead of under guard. In those days my curiosity had been stunted. So many unusual things went on about me all the time I had lost my sense of interest in anything that did not actually concern me. But something seemed to hold my attention to this strange looking company.

I got up from the ground where I was sitting and went to the edge of our camp to watch the soldiers passing. The first lines went by. The Armenian women came nearer. Suddenly all the world about me seemed lost in a haze. I rushed in between the horses, screaming at the top of my voice:

"Mother! Mother! Mother!"

She heard, and little Hovnan, and Mardiros, and Sarah heard. Mother slid to the ground as I ran up to her. I tried to throw my arms around her neck, while my little brothers and sister clung to me. But mother caught my arms and held them. Her eyes were closed, and she was still and silent. I cried to her to speak to me. A terrible fear came over me. Had she gone mad? Had she lost her speech?

I screamed — this time with anguish. Mother opened her eyes.

"Be patient, my daughter," she said, with the dear, sweet gentleness for which all our friends had loved her. "Be patient, my daughter. I was just talking with God — thanking Him that my prayers have come true!" When I had kissed and cried over Hovnan and Mardiros and Sarah, I looked again into mother's face.

Little Aruciag — she was not there. Mother saw the question in my eyes.

"Aruciag has gone. She grew tired one day and could not keep up. A soldier threw her over a precipice!"

An officer of the hamidieh came up to learn what was happening, why mother and the children had dismounted to stand in the way of the horsemen. Mother explained to him that I was her daughter, who had come back to her. She said she wished that I might travel with her. The officer was kind. He gave permission and promised to send another donkey for me to ride.

There were four young Armenian girls with mothers and several older women, whose faces bore the marks of much suffering. As we rode along mother explained to me.

When I was stolen from her and our party from Tchemesh-Gedzak, so many weeks before, she was lying at the roadside, cruelly wounded by the soldiers. But the thought of the children summoned her back to life. Friends cared for her, and the next day when the company moved on, they carried her in their arms until she could walk again.

She passed Malatia, Geulik and Diyarbekir. At last she reached Ourfa. By this time only eighteen were left of the original four thousand exiles from Tchemesh-Gedzak.

At Ourfa there lived my uncle, mother's cousin, Ipranos Mardiganian, who had moved from Tchemesh-Gedzak to Ourfa many years ago — before I was born. Uncle Ipranos had become very wealthy, and had established a great trading business, which had branches even in Persia and in Constantinople.

In the Abdul-Hamid massacres of 1895 Uncle Ipranos was persuaded by his powerful Turkish friends at Constantinople and in Ourfa to become Moslem and thus save his life. He pretended to do so, and was rewarded with a government position of high trust, and rose to high estate among the Moslems. He adopted a Turkish name, and was known as Ibrahim Agha. Secretly, though, he still prayed to God and was Christian.

Mother remembered him when she reached Ourfa with the refugees. She knew he was in the favor of the Turks, who no longer looked upon him as Armenian. She asked one of the soldiers with her party if he would take a letter into the city for her, promising that if he would deliver the letter secretly, he would receive pay. The soldier took the letter to Ibrahim Agha's house. In it, mother appealed to her cousin for his assistance in the name of their family, and asked him to give some money to the soldier.

Ibrahim Agha was grieved by mother's letter. He sent her word that he would help her. He went at once to Haidar Pasha and procured his permission to bring mother and her children to his house. Then he came for her and took her to his home. In his house mother found four Armenian girls. Their mothers were deported from Ourfa, but before they had left the city, they had appealed to Ibrahim Agha to take their daughters under his protection, thinking to save them. He could not refuse, although he endangered his own life, and had to keep the girls hidden from his neighbors. A few older women also were in his house, hidden in his cellar. He had taken them in from the streets when soldiers were not looking.

For more than a month, mother and the children were safe in her cousin's home. Then, one day, Haidar Pasha sent him word to come to the government building. He returned with heavy heart. Haidar Pasha had told him it would not be safe for him to keep his relatives in his house any longer; that many high military officials were in Ourfa, and if some of them should hear of refugee Armenians being thus protected, all might be killed, and both he and Ibrahim Agha suffer.

But Haidar Pasha offered to obtain from the Turkish general at Aleppo, military permission for mother and the children and the other exiles in his house, of whom my uncle now told him, to travel back to their homes in the north with soldiers being sent to Moush to join the campaign against the Russians. For this Haidar Pasha asked one thousand liras cash — about $5,000 — and another thousand liras when mother and the others had safely reached their homes and had received permission from their home authorities to remain. This permission the Pasha promised to arrange also.

My uncle had to comply. The four girls had no homes or relatives in the north, but they had to go, too, or be deported and seized by Turks. Mother agreed to take them to her home in Tchemesh-Gedzak — if they should really reach there alive.

At Moush an army corps was assembling. The Turks had retired before the first advance of the Russians through the Caucasus, and Djevdet Bey, Vali of Van, was rallying his armies here for a dash at the Russian flanks, which already had reached Van. Soldiers occupied all the houses in Moush, from which the Armenians had been ejected, and the hamidieh officers believed it would be best for us to be quartered outside the city while arrangements were made for the rest of our journey. Mother depended upon the papers given her by Haidar Pasha to secure for us an escort from Moush to Tchemesh-Gedzak — and Ibrahim Agha had said Haidar would telegraph the authorities at Moush to guarantee our safety.

We stopped at Kurdmeidan, a village a few miles outside of Moush, at the foot of Mount Antok. There had been many Armenians in the village, and there was an Armenian church. All the Christians had been massacred, however, and their homes were occupied by mouhajirs — Moslem immigrants from the lost provinces in the Balkans. We went into the deserted church and prepared to remain there until arrangements were made for us to leave. The hamidieh officers called the village Mudir before them and cautioned him that we were to be protected and fed — that we were "especially favored by the Porte."

The villagers treated us kindly — so great is the fear of the population of anything "official" or governmental. Days went by and we did not hear from the city. We began to worry. Mother wanted so much to see our home again at Tchemesh-Gedzak. "Were it not for you and the children," she would say to me, "I would be willing to die on my doorstep — if God would just let me see our home again!" My poor, dear mother!

We dared not go alone into the city to inquire what was to be done for us — we could only wait.

One night, just after the Moslem prayer, the streets of the little city suddenly became crowded with horsemen. Some Turkish women who were just outside the church rushed in to get out of the way of the horses' hoofs. "It is Sheikh Zilan," they said. "The Sheikh Zilan of the Belek tribe, who has been called in from the mountains with his thousand Kurds to fight for the Turks!"

The name of Sheikh Zilan was widely known. His horsemen had harried the countryside for many years. It was said he frequently made raids with his tribe into Persia, and even into the Russian Caucasus before the war, to steal women for the secret slave markets in European Turkey.

The tribe was on its way into Moush. Entrance would be denied them after dark, they knew, so they had decided to camp for the night in Kurdmeidan. Some followers of the Sheikh saw the Armenian church building, and decided to use it as a stable for the horses of the Sheikh and his chiefs. They broke in the door while mother and the rest of us crouched in a corner. But we could not hide — the Kurds saw us and gave the alarm. Soon the church was full of the wild tribesmen.

Mother showed her letters from Haidar Pasha. This awed the Kurds for a moment, and they sent for one of their chiefs. When the chief came, he read the letter carefully. Then he examined our party. "The Pasha here says there is an Armenian woman and her servants and three children, to whom immunity has been promised and safe conduct. That we will grant, although the word of a Pasha is not binding upon the will of the great Shiekh Zilan. But the Pasha's writing says nothing of five young Armenian women, too old to be classed as children and too young to be described as servants. These we will take, lest the Pasha be imposed upon."

They would not believe that I also was mother's daughter. They took me and the four girls mother had brought from the house of Ibrahim Agha, and at the same time forced mother to leave the shelter of the church and camp in a nearby yard. They took us out of the village, to where their main camp was.

With halter ropes they tied our hands behind our backs and then tied us to each other by looping a rope through our arms. Soon Sheikh Zilan himself came to look at us. He seemed greatly pleased

142

when he had looked into our faces. He gave some orders we could not understand, but which, evidently, had to do with our safety, and walked away. We spent the night sitting on the ground, for we were bound in such a way we could not lie down. The Kurds looked at us curiously as they walked around us, and often one of them would kick us to make us turn our faces toward him. But otherwise they did not molest us.

XIII

OLD VARTABED AND THE SHEPHERD'S CALL

EARLY in the morning we were taken into the city, tied across horses which were led just behind the group of chiefs who followed Sheikh Zilan, himself. Inside the city four horsemen led our horses into one of the low quarters of the city. Here we were given into the keeping of a cruel looking Kurd, whom I was soon to know was Bekran Agha, the notorious slave dealer of Moush.

Ten thousand Armenian girls, delicate, refined daughters of Christian homes, college girls, young school teachers, daughters of the rich and the poor, have experienced the terror of the same feeling that came over me that day when I realized that I was a captive in the house of this notorious slave dealer. His slave market had been boldly operated, in the security of his house, for many years, but never had he enjoyed such a profitable trade as when the Armenian girls were available to him.

Bekran left us in his donkey stable at night. In the morning his hammal came in to feed the animals. When he had finished this task, he ordered us to follow him.

Bekran awaited us in his selamlik. I shuddered when I saw him — he was so old and withered and cruel looking. A negress waited upon him. He sat on the floor in the old fashion. The selamlik was barren and ill-kept. Everywhere there was dirt. Bekran's flowing garments, once of rich texture, were ragged and frayed. Yet I knew Bekran must be very rich — from the profits the helplessness of Armenians had brought him.

We fell upon our knees before him — then we bent into the posture of the Mohammedans — we wanted so much to make him listen to our pleading. I had suffered so much, I thought surely I could persuade this old man to let me go to my mother again. But Bekran did not even speak. His eyes roved over us — I could feel them. He signed to the hammal and the man lifted us to our feet, one by one, that his master might see our height, our size and judge of our attractiveness. Then he gave another sign and we were taken across the inside court, through a stone doorway, and into a large room where there were a number of other Armenian girls, with here and there a Circassian or a Russian from the Caucasus, among them.

Soon the hammal came into the room with figs and bread. I could not eat, neither could any of the four girls who had been of my mother's party from Ourfa. Few of the others ate, either — as all had come but recently into the hands of Bekran and were too downcast. When the hammal saw that we, who were late comers, did not eat, he said, "That is well. We will lose no time at the bath." He then compelled us to cleanse ourselves as well as we could of the marks of our nights in the sand and in the donkey stable with water from a fountain in the courtyard.

Two men servants who came into the court while we were bathing joined the hammal. Together they made us stand in a long line. The girls who had been in the house when we arrived, saved us from the whips the hammal and his men carried by telling us what to do.

We were taken into a large room at the back of the house, barren of any furniture, save a pile of cushions on a rug in one corner. We were allowed to sit on the floor any place in the room, but in this corner where the cushions were. Before long Bekran Agha came in and sat on the cushions.

All morning purchasers came. As each one spoke to Bekran, the porter would clap his hands and we were made to gather in a circle around the customer. Many girls were sold — but for only a few pennies apiece. There were too many in the market to demand large prices! When a girl was sold, she remained until a servant came to take her away.

Late in the afternoon of the second day, a customer to whom Bekran Agha paid great deference, entered the room. He was a servant, but from his clothes I knew him to be the servant of a rich man. From those of us who were left he selected three — and I was one of the three. While we stood near, he bargained with Bekran. At last the terms were agreed upon. I was bought for one medjidieh — 85 cents!

Outside was an araba. The other two girls and I were placed in this. We were taken outside the city, to a country house occupied by Djevdet Bey, Vali of Van, then commander of the Turkish army operating against the Russians.

We were taken at once to the haremlik, where there were a number of other young Armenian women. Before evening the kalfa, or head servant, came in to us and we were asked, one by one, if we were willing to become Mohammedans. The kalfa explained that only those could remain in the care and keeping of Djevdet Bey, the mighty man, and have the honor of his protection, who willingly adopted the creed of Islam.

Though he was cruel and, as his deeds show, the most unscrupulous of all the Turks, Djevdet Bey desired, it was made plain to us, to keep within the provisions of the fetva issued by Abdul Hamid and still in effect, which pretends to prohibit the enslaving of Armenian and other Christian girls unless they first become Mohammedans.

I did not know what the kalfa would do with me if I refused to accept the creed of Islam. I feared the punishment would be death, or the public khan at once, but I could not bring myself to deny Christ, after having remained faithful to Him so long. I asked Him what I should do — and His answer came, just as clear and direct as when I was about to use my knife outside the rocks of Diyarbekir. I seemed to see Father Rhoupen, the priest, and I even felt his hand on my shoulder again, just as when he said to me, "Always trust in God and remain faithful unto Him." I told the kalfa I could not forswear Jesus Christ.

One of the other girls who had been brought to Djevdet Bey's house with me also refused to give up her religion, even to save her life. The third girl had suffered so much — her heart and soul were broken. She gave way. The kalfa put her into another room. In a little while we who had refused to apostatize were summoned, put into separate arabas, and driven away. What became of the other little girl I do not know. I was taken to the house of Ahmed Bey, one of the rich men of Moush. I was a present to him from Djevdet Bey.

I cannot forget the depression that came over me when I entered the courtyard of Ahmed Bey's house. Twice before, since the deportations began, had I been taken a captive into the houses of Turks and left at their mercy. Yet now I felt as if the future were darker than ever before. Perhaps it was because the house of Ahmed was outside the city, in the plains — as a prison would be. And there were twenty-four other girls in the haremlik, each with her own memory of sufferings, more terrible even, some of them, than had been my own.

Ahmed Bey, himself, was very old, yet some of these twenty-four girls had been sacrificed to him. The others had been divided between his two sons. Ahmed was, perhaps, a truer type of the fanatical Turk than any whose victim I had yet been. His interest seemed not to be so much in the young women themselves, as in the children he wanted them to bear to his sons — children in whom the blood of the noble Armenian race might be blended with that of the savage Turk, and who might live to perpetuate and improve the blood of his family.

I was summoned before Ahmed Bey the next day. I had asked for clothing, but the haremlik attaches would not give me any, nor would they allow me to accept garments from other girls in the harem. "Not until Ahmed indicates his desires," was the answer of the kalfa to my pleadings.

Ahmed Bey spoke to me gently, but it was with the gentleness that hurts worse than blows. "You are to be one of the favored of my women," he said, "because you have been sent to my house by His Excellency, Djevdet Bey." He gave a sign, and a little slave girl appeared with the rich dress of a favored Turkish girl. "Many of these and many ornaments, as well as kindness and affection, shall be yours as long as you are obedient and respectful," Ahmed said. "First, you shall renounce the Christ you have been taught to worship and accept the forgiveness of Allah and Mohammed, his prophet."

I told him I was weary of suffering, but that I had been given into the keeping of God by my mother, and that I would not desert Him. At this Ahmed became furious. All his gentleness passed away. He trembled in his anger. He upbraided me and my people and blasphemed my religion. I cried with shame at hearing him, but he had no pity. I pleaded with him to free me, that I might return to my mother's party, and I told him of the paper given my mother by Haidar Pasha of Ourfa. But he would not listen.

The little slave was sent from the room to summon one of Ahmed's sons. The son came in almost immediately. Ahmed called him "Nazim." "This is the one sent me by Djevdet Bey, himself. I have set her aside for you, my son, because of her comeliness and youth. But her spirit must be broken. I have sent for you that you might look upon her and decide — what shall be done with her."

Ahmed's son spoke to me, but I did not answer. Then he took my hand, drew me up before him and lifted my face that he might look into my eyes.

"Leave her to me, my father, that I may try to persuade her to be happy in our house," Nazim said.

The little slave led me to an apartment — a small room looking out upon an inside court, with a divan. I asked her to leave the dress with me, that I might at least cover myself, but she said she could not do that without permission. When she had left me Nazim crossed the court from the selamlik and came at once to me.

He had the same gentleness as his father — and it hurt in the same way. He asked me to accept Mohammed that he might make me his "bride." He told me my sufferings would be very hard to bear if I refused, but that I would have many luxuries if I consented.

I knew I could not escape. My thoughts went to my mother. I told Nazim that as long as my mother was an exile, doomed to die a wanderer, I could not speak of being a "bride." I told him if he would save her, if he would bring her to me, I would ask her if she thought best that I sacrifice my religion in return for my life and safety — and if she would say it would be right, then, with her always near to comfort me, I would let my soul die that my body and hers might live.

"You will have to learn it is not the slave's privilege to bargain," he said, as he strode away.

Hours went by, and I crouched on the divan — waiting. At every step I feared I was to be summoned again — this time for something I could only expect to be torture. At last a zaptieh who was one of Ahmed Bey's personal retainers came for me. He lifted me roughly and dragged me with him across the court and into the road in front of the house. A little way from the garden wall there was a group of other zaptiehs.

Among them I saw my mother, little Hovnan and Mardiros and little Sarah, my brothers and sister, and the others of my mother's party. I had told Nazim where they were when I pleaded with him to restore them to me — and he had sent for them.

I tried to break away, to run toward them. The zaptieh at my side held me. My mother was kneeling, with her hands lifted to heaven. Sarah ran toward me, her arms stretched out. "Aurora — Aurora — don't let them kill us!" Sarah cried. The zaptieh swung the heavy handle of his whip high in the air and brought it down on Sarah's head so that the blow flung her little body far out of the path. She did not move again. I think the blow must have crushed in my little sister's head.

Mother saw — and so did Hovnan and Mardiros. Mother fell to the ground, motionless. A zaptieh lifted her and struck her with his whip.

I fell upon my knees before the chief of the zaptiehs. "Spare my mother — spare my brothers!" I cried to him. "I will do anything you wish — I will belong to Allah — I will thank him only — if you will spare them!"

"It shall be as Nazim Bey desires," the zaptieh said. I did not understand — I clung to him and prayed to him. I tried to touch my mother, but the zaptieh kicked me to the ground. Then, suddenly, I knew why they waited. Nazim Bey had come out of the house. When I saw him, I crept to his feet and begged him for mercy. "I will be Turkish — I will pray to Allah — I will obey — just to save my mother," I cried to him.

"That is well — but you shall not only be a Moslem but you also shall be the daughter of a Moslem — that will be better still" — said Nazim. "What does the old woman say?"

A zaptieh jerked mother to her feet again. He lifted his whip. "The creed — quick!" he said to her.

"Mother, please — God will forgive you — father is in heaven and he will understand!" I cried to her.

Mother was too weak to speak aloud, but her lips moved in a whisper: "God of St. Gregory, Thy will be done!"

The zaptieh's heavy whip descended. Mother sank to the ground. I tried to reach her, but the zaptiehs held me. I fought them, but they held me fast. Again and again the whip fell. Mardiros screamed and tried to save her with his weak little hands. Another zaptieh caught him by the arm and killed him with a single blow from his whip handle. When they flung him aside, Mardiros's body fell almost at my feet.

Hovnan wrapped his arms around the zaptieh who was beating my mother, but his strength was too feeble. The zaptieh did not even notice him until my mother's body relaxed and I knew she was dead. Then he drew his knife and plunged it into little Hovnan.

It was only a little while — two minutes, perhaps, or three, that I stood there, held by the zaptieh. But in those short minutes all that belonged to me in this world was swept away — my mother, Mardiros and Hovnan, and Sarah. Their bodies were at my feet. Both mother and Hovnan died with their eyes turned to me, looking into mine! My eyes see them now, every day and every night — every hour, almost — when I look out into the new world about me. I must keep them closed for hours at a time to shut the vision out.

I heard Nazim Bey give an order to his zaptiehs. Some of them picked up the bodies of my dear ones and carried them away, I do not know where. The others lifted me off the ground — I could not walk — and carried me to the house and back to the room where the divan was. For two days and nights no one came near me but the slave girls. All that time I cried; I could not keep the tears from coming. That was when my eyes gave way; that is why I cannot see very well now without glasses.

On the third day Nazim, accompanied by his father, Ahmed, came to my room. Ahmed spoke with the same cruel gentleness. "What is past is gone, little one; it is time your thoughts should turn to the future. Nazim desires you. You are honored. He has punished you for your stubbornness, and he would forgive you and take you to his heart. That is as it must be. Your people are gone. There is none to give you mistaken counsel. You will now accept the favor of Allah and enter into a state of true righteousness."

"I want to die — kill me! I will never listen to your son nor to your Allah," I said.

They took me into another wing of the house, to a dungeon room, with just one iron-barred window looking out into the courtyard. There was no divan or cushions, just the floor and the walls. The window was high in the wall. I could not look out at anything but the sky — that same sky which covered so much of tragedy in my ravished Armenia.

THE ROADSIDE OF AWFUL DESPAIR
First the children died, and then the parents, and uncles and aunts. The grieving parents wrapped the little ones in the sheets they had brought along, and then lay down beside them to starve. It was a

151

common scene in the deserts and along the sandy roads over which the exiles travelled.

Day after day, night after night, went by. Each day the alaiks came and brought me bread, berries and milk. And each day the hodja, a teacher-priest, came to ask me if I were ready to accept Islam. But each day God took me closer into His heart, for I kept up my courage by talking to Him.

And then one night, after so many days had passed I had lost count of them, God reached in through my dungeon window. I was awakened by a commotion in the courtyard, where, on other nights, it had been very quiet. Soon I understood what was happening — sheep were being driven in through the gate. Ahmed's flock was coming in from the hill pastures, driven in, perhaps, by military conditions.

I heard the yard gates swing shut. Then, above the bleating of the excited, restless sheep, I heard the shepherd whistle his call to quiet them. I jumped to my feet, my heart throbbing. Breathlessly I listened for the shepherd to repeat the call. Then I was sure — it was the same peculiar call, sharp and shrill, which my father always taught his own shepherds, the call which he had been taught by his own father when, as a little boy, he learned the ways of his father's sheep on the great pastures of Mamuret-ul-Aziz. When I was very young our shepherds used to laugh at me when I tried to imitate them. I had been a very happy little girl when, one day, I succeeded so well that suddenly the sheep in our flock turned away from their grass and came toward me.

No other shepherds than ours or, at least, one who had come from Tchemesh-Gedzak, would know that call, I was certain. Ahmed's sheep were tired and nervous. The unknown shepherd remained among them, every now and then repeating that same whistle, softer and softer. I went close to the window, lifted my face toward the iron-barred window and repeated the call. Even the sheep seemed to sense something unusual. They were suddenly quiet. Again I whistled, this time with more courage. Instantly the shepherd answered — I could almost detect his note of wonder.

I had learned that by leaping as high as I could I could catch the window bars with my hands and lift myself until my face reached above the window-sill. Often I had caught glimpses of the yard in this way. But I was not strong enough to hold myself up more than a few seconds at a time.

Now I tried this, hoping to catch a glimpse of the shepherd in the moonlight. As I pulled myself up, I whistled again. Many times I tried before I attracted his attention to the window. When I had succeeded and he understood that behind that window there was a captive who was trying to signal him, he made me understand by repeating his whistle three times in quick succession directly under the window.

I dared not call out to him. I tore a great piece of cloth from the dress that had been given me. I rolled this into a ball and threw it out. He saw and answered by whistling softly. I hoped he would understand the torn cloth as a symbol of my imprisonment — and of my hope that he would save me. I could hardly believe that even an Armenian shepherd would be left alive, yet it seemed to be so.

In the morning when the sheep were taken out the shepherd whistled again under my window and I knew he was trying to attract my attention. I answered as softly as I could. All that day a new hope gave me courage. I was sure deliverance was at hand, though I could not explain why.

I did not even attempt to sleep that night. The sheep came in early and the shepherd whistled. An hour later I heard the call again — the shepherd still was in the yard. It must have been near midnight when I heard a rattling at the window bars. I looked, and there, framed in the moonlight, was a face I knew — the face of Old Vartabed, who had come to our house that Easter morning with his prophecy of ill — the prophecy that came true. God had sent him to me and had made me to hear and understand that familiar, whistled call!

Old Vartabed whispered: "Who is here who comes from the Mamuret-ul-Aziz?"

"It is Aurora, the daughter of the Mardiganians of Tchemesh-Gedzak. You are Old Vartabed, and I am the Aurora you loved so much."

Old Vartabed tried to speak, but his voice shook so I could not understand him. I told him all that I could, quickly. How I had come to be a captive of Ahmed and why I was in the dungeon. Tears came into Old Vartabed's ancient eyes when I told him how all my people were dead. I asked him how it was that he had been saved. "Old Vartabed is not worth the slaughter," he said. "I am of much value, since I have taught the sheep of Ahmed to behave only for me. Ahmed has forgotten I am an Armenian, since I bend my knees for every prayer to Allah and thus prolong my days." He told me to be patient. He would find a way to save me.

XIV

THE MESSAGE OF GENERAL ANDRANIK

Two nights went by before Old Vartabed came again. But each night he signaled and I answered. On the third night, his face was framed again in the window casement.

"Be ready, little one — I shall lift you out soon," he whispered. He had brought a steel bar with which to pry aside the iron bars in the window. The bars were very old — perhaps for a hundred years or more they had served to shut in the prisoners that once had been confined in this same dungeon room in Ahmed Bey's big house. I knelt to pray, and I was on my knees when Vartabed whispered:

"Come, little one — reach Old Vartabed your hand — he will lift you."

The bars were bent aside. There was room for the shepherd to lean inward and reach down. I caught his hands and he lifted me until I could catch hold of the iron and help myself. In a moment I leaped down to the stump which the shepherd had brought to stand on, and from this to the ground. The sheep, which were resting all about, stirred and bleated when I fell among them, but Old Vartabed whistled and they were quiet.

"We must go quickly; the gate is not locked. You must be far away, to a place I will tell you of, before morning comes and you are missed," Old Vartabed said as he hurried me across the yard.

When we were outside the gate, Old Vartabed wrapped his coat around me, for it was cold. Then we struck out across the plains, away from the town and toward low hills in the distance.

Old Vartabed did not talk much. He was so old he needed his strength. He was anxious that I get far away before dawn. When we came to the hills, the shepherd showed me a path and told me to follow it, and go on alone until I came to the hut of a friendly Kurdish family.

"But you, Old Vartabed — are you not coming with me? Will not Ahmed Bey suspect you if you return?" I asked.

"Old Vartabed is too old to live in the desert, and then, who would care for my sheep?" the old man replied.

Poor, dear Old Vartabed! Ahmed Bey had him killed in the morning.

I ran along the path the shepherd pointed out to me until, after many hours, I came to the hut of the Kurds, of whom Old Vartabed had told me. They were shepherd Kurds, and had great respect for Old Vartabed, who had told them I was the daughter of his one-time master in the Mamuret-ul-Aziz. They expected me, and were very kind.

When I thought of Old Vartabed going back to his sheep, and to the mercy of Ahmed Bey, I cried. The shepherd Kurd's wife and daughters were sorry, and the Kurd himself went down toward the plain in which Ahmed's house stood, to learn if Old Vartabed still tended his sheep. That night he came back in great distress. He had learned of Old Vartabed's fate. None but the shepherd could have helped me escape, Ahmed Bey had been sure. He had summoned Old Vartabed before him and the shepherd had confessed, as there was no other way. Ahmed Bey sent for his zaptiehs. Old Vartabed was led out to where his flock was waiting to be taken to the pasture. There was a shot, and he had paid with his life for his kindness to the little daughter of his one-time master.

The Kurd was much alarmed for me. Ahmed Bey had sent zaptiehs to search in the plains and hills. Perhaps they would soon be at the hut.

They would not send me away, but I knew that I must go. The hut was too close to the house of Ahmed, and the zaptiehs might come when least expected. So they gave me woolen stockings, the best they had, a great loaf of winter bread, a jug in which to carry water, and a blanket to wrap about me at night. Then I went out into the hills.

Beyond these hills was the great Dersim — the highlands of grass and sand, with hills and mountains everywhere. For many, many miles in each direction no one lived but Dersim Kurds, some in little villages, some in roving bands. On each side of the Dersim lived the Turks. Once Armenians lived in the cities of the Turks, but now the Armenians all were gone — only Turks were left.

The inhabitants of the Dersim deserts and wastes are not the vicious type of Kurds who live in the south in the regions to which we had been deported from our homes. The Kurds in the south are nomadic tribes, harsh and cruel. The Dersim Kurds mostly are farmers, and often rebel against their Turkish overlords. They are fanatical Moslems, and have their racial hatred of all "unbelievers," as they look upon Christians. But they do not have the lust of killing human beings common with the tribes of the south. To this I owe my life.

For more than a year I was a captive or a wanderer in the Dersim. For many days after I left my friends at the news of Old Vartabed's fate I hid in the daytime and traveled at night, walking, walking, always walking; somewhere, and yet nowhere. When a settlement loomed up before me, I turned the other way, trudging aimlessly across the wide plains, through the hills or over deserts.

My bread soon gave out, and water was hard to get, for wherever there was a well or a spring a settlement of Kurds was close. Near one well I hid throughout one whole day, waiting my chance to slip up unobserved and cool my parched throat. There was no opportunity in the daylight, and when night came and I gathered courage to creep near to the well, the dogs from the houses ran out and barked at me. I was too exhausted to run when the villagers came out to see what had aroused the dogs. They took me into the settlement and shut me up in a cave for the night. In the morning the chief of the settlement took me as his slave and commanded me to obey the orders of his family.

They made me do the work a man would do. I tended the stock, carried the water and worked in the fields. When I did not do enough work, the Kurds would beat me with their long, thick sticks and refuse me food. When I did enough work to please them, the women would throw me a piece of bread. At night I slept on the ground, outside the huts, with rags and torn blankets to keep out the cold, but never was I warm.

After weeks passed, I was too weak to work any longer. I fell down when I went to the fields, and could not get up when a Kurd kicked me. So they gave me half a loaf of bread and told me to go away. I went a little way and then rested for two days. It was so nice not to have to drag a plow made of sticks from morning to night, I soon got my strength back. And then I started to walk again.

Beyond Erzerum I knew there were Russians — friends of the Armenians. I tried to keep my face turned to where I thought Erzerum would be — a hundred miles or more through the Dersim. I kept away from the villages until I could walk no more for want of food or water. Then I would give myself up to be a work slave again. Each time the Kurds kept me until my strength gave way. Then they gave me the half loaf of bread and let me go away.

Although it was very cold now, I had no clothes. The Kurds would never let me have any of the cloth they spun. Snow in the crevices among the hills gave me water, but all I had to cat for weeks, even months, at a time was the bark from small trees, weeds that grow in the winter time, and the dead blades of grass I found under the snow.

The snow had melted when I reached the edge of the Dersim to the west. I do not know what month it was, as I had lost all track of time, but I knew spring was passing because the snow disappeared. I was now in the neighborhood of Turkish cities. Occasionally I saw Turks, in their white coats, walking over the plains. I saw flocks of sheep now and then, and other signs that I was near cities. Yet I knew I must keep away from these cities or their inhabitants.

One day from the side of a hill where I was hiding, almost too weak from hunger to walk, I saw a great line of people with donkeys and carts and arabas, passing on what seemed to be a road to the south. As far as I could see, this cavalcade stretched out. For hours it wound its way across the plains. I wondered what it meant. I crept down from the hill and, crawling on the ground, drew as near as I could. I saw the people were Turks, and that they were carrying household goods with them. I saw, too, that they were excited and seemed to be unhappy.

I watched the line of Turkish families go by all day. When it was dark, I determined to go the way they had come from. Whatever it was that had sent the Turks from their homes in the cities further east, it could not be anything that meant ill for a girl of the Armenians.

Already I had crossed the Kara River, the farthest branch of the Euphrates. Along the roads over which the Turks had passed in the daytime, there were scraps of bread, glass jars from which fruits had been emptied, and other remnants of food. I gathered enough to give me strength for walking.

The plains across which I made my way that night were those which once formed the Garden of Eden, according to the teachings of the priests and our Sunday school books. The Kara River was one of the Four Rivers. Nearby were the Acampis of the Bible and the Chorok and the Aras, the other three. Among these same rocks through which I hurried along as fast as my strength would allow, Eve herself once had wandered. When I sat down at times to rest, I thought of Eve, and wondered if she were some place Up Above, looking down upon me, one of the last of the great race of people which had been the first to accept the teachings of Christ and which had suffered so much in His name through all the centuries that have passed since Eve's gardens blossomed on the plains and slopes about me.

The next day there were more lines of Turkish refugees. These appeared to be belated and hurried in great confusion. Turkish soldiers appeared among them, and there were many zaptiehs. Far beyond, I saw the minarets of a city. I knew it must be Erzerum. I came near to a village and saw the inhabitants rushing about from house to house in excitement.

I was afraid to travel in the daytime. I could not go near one of these villages, even to beg for water, because I had no clothes, and would be ashamed, even if I dared to trust that I would not be taken captive. During the night I crept closer to the distant city. In the morning I stood at the edge of a plateau, which broke downward in a sheer drop to the plain. Clinging close to rocks, which hid me from the view of the refugees who still passed along the roads, I could look down into the city.

I saw a great rushing about. Moving bodies of soldiers came and went. Refugees were streaming out of the city and were joined by others from villages all around. In the distance I could hear what I knew to be the firing of guns.

The firing came closer. Now and then big guns spoke, shaking the ground about me. I saw explosions in the city. Houses appeared to fall each time the big guns sounded. Far across the city there suddenly appeared clouds of dust. They drew nearer. Soldiers fled out of the gates of the city nearest me, in the wake of the civilians.

Late in the afternoon the firing ceased. The dust clouds beyond the city had drawn closer. Out of them suddenly emerged bands of horsemen. They rode directly toward the far gates. Companies of Turkish soldiers met them at the city walls. There was a clash. The Turks were driven back. The horsemen followed. There was rifle firing. Other bands of horsemen rode down from every direction in the east, in through the gates and into the city itself.

The Russians had come!

In an hour the city was almost quiet again. Far off I saw great columns of troops moving slowly. Behind the Cossacks, the Russian army was coming. The Turks in the city had surrendered.

When night fell, I went down from the rocks and into the town. I hoped before dawn came I could find a garment, or a piece of shawl, which had been thrown away and with which I could cover myself. Terror of the Cossacks kept indoors the citizens who had been brave enough to remain in their homes. The streets were deserted in the outskirts, except for an occasional zaptieh stealing along, as afraid to be seen as I was.

Suddenly, as I turned the corner of a narrow street, hugging close to the wall, hoping that this turn, or the next, would bring me near one of the houses I knew the Russians must have occupied, I saw a beautiful sight — the American flag. The rays of a searchlight played on it.

Lights shone from all the windows in the house over which the flag flew. There, I knew, would be my haven of safety. But not until after the dawn did I have the courage to go near. Then I saw the figures of men moving about the yard and near the doorways. I ran out of my hiding place and fell at the feet of a tall, kindly-looking man, who had just emerged from the house door, and who stood talking to a Russian officer.

I felt the tall man stoop down and put his hand upon my head. All at once the sun seemed to break out of the gray dawn and shine down upon me. Then I fell asleep. When I opened my eyes again it was many days after, they told me. I was in a warm bed, and kindly people were all about me. When they spoke to me in a strange language, I tried to ask for the tall man who had lifted me up from the street at the doorstep. An interpreter came, and then, in a little while, the tall man came in and smiled gently, and I knew that everything was all right.

This man, they told me, was a famous missionary physician, Dr. F. W. MacCallum, who was known for his kindnesses to my people throughout the Turkish empire. He had been compelled to leave Constantinople when the war came, but he had come into Erzerum with the Russians — to be among the first to give succor to my people. The house had once been the American mission. The missionaries had been compelled to flee, but they had returned with the Russians.

Dr. MacCallum, who now is in New York and was the first good friend I found after my arrival in this country, bought thousands of Armenian girls out of slavery in those days when the Russians were pushing into Turkey from the Caucasus. With money supplied by the American Committee for Armenian and Syrian Relief, he purchased these girls from their Turkish captors for $1 apiece. The Turks, knowing the Russians would liberate these captive Christian girls if they found them, were glad to sell them at this price rather than risk losing them without collecting anything.

General Andranik, the great Armenian leader, who is our national hero, came to see me. For many years General Andranik kept alive the courage of all Armenians. He promised them freedom and constantly endangered his life to keep up the spirits of my people. The Turks put a price upon his head, and he was hunted from one end of the empire to the other — yet he always escaped. He led the Armenian regiments, made up of Armenians who lived in Russia, in the vanguard of the Russian army sent against the Turks.

When I told General Andranik how I had seen my own dear people killed, he felt very sorry for me. He comforted and cheered me, and called me his "little girl." I would rather he said that to me than give me all the riches in the world.

A Russian officer who could speak Armenian also came to talk with me. When I had told him everything he left, but in an hour he returned. This time a very distinguished looking officer, very tall, with a kind face, came with him. I knew he must be of very high rank, for there was much excitement when he entered the house. The officer who had talked with me first repeated to the other many of the things I had told him. The distinguished looking officer then spoke to me, first in Russian, and then in French, which I understood.

"You have been a very unhappy girl," he said, "and I am very happy to have arrived in time to save you. We shall take good care of you, and all Russians will be your friends."

When he had gone, they told me who he was — the Grand Duke, in command of the armies in the Caucasus. The officer who had visited me first was General Trokin, the Grand Duke's chief of staff.

When I was well and strong, General Andranik allowed me to help care for hundreds of Armenian children who had been found in the hands of the Turks and Armenian refugees who had succeeded in hiding in the hills and mountains and who now crept in to ask protection of the Russians. I helped, too, to comfort the girls who had been bought out of the harems.

When General Andranik moved on with the advancing Russians, the Grand Duke ordered that I be escorted safely to Sari Kamish, where the railroad begins, and sent from there to Tiflis, the capital of the Russian Caucasus. When General Andranik bade me good-by he said:

"The Grand Duke has indorsed arrangements for you to be sent to America, where our poor Armenians have many friends. When you reach that beloved land, tell its people that Armenia is prostrate, torn and bleeding, but that it will rise again — if America will only help us — send food for the starving, and money to take them back to their homes when the war is over."

As I started away with the escort, toward Sari Kamish, General Andranik took from his finger a beautiful ring, which, he said, had been his father's and his grandfather's, and put it on my finger. It is the ring I wear now — all that is left to me of my country.

From Sari Kamish the Grand Duke's soldiers sent me to Tiflis. There I was received by representatives of the American Committee for Armenian and Syrian Relief, and supplied with funds sufficient to take me, with the Grand Duke's passport, to Petrograd, Sweden and America.

But when I reached Petrograd all was not well within the city. Already the Czar had been removed and the government of Minister Kerensky was losing control of the populace. Rioting in the streets had begun, and the authorities to whom the Grand Duke and the American representatives at Tiflis had sent me had been removed or executed.

Again I was friendless and without shelter. I had a great deal of money, but I could buy hardly any food. For fifty rubles I could purchase only a loaf of bread. When I became so hungry, I stopped kind looking persons in the street to ask them if they could help me obtain something to eat, they would look at me sorrowfully, offer me handful of paper money, and say they could give me that, but not food. Everyone seemed to have a great deal of money, but things to eat were very scarce.

No one dared take me in. I found an Armenian church, empty now and deserted. All the Armenians who had lived in Petrograd had been frightened away. They had been the first, because of their experiences in their own country, to scent the coming of trouble, and had disappeared. I remained in the deserted church for many days, afraid to go out in the streets, where there was much killing and robbery. Only in the early morning, when the streets were more quiet, would I venture to look for food.

At last I saw an American passing the church. I ran out and begged him, in French, to help me. I showed him my passport and he took me in a droschky to the American Embassy. Here every one was kind to me. My passports were changed and the next day I was started toward Christiania.

The train on which I traveled was stopped many times by bands of soldiers, who demanded the passports of every one. Although they took several persons from the train at one stop, my passport was honored and I went on. The farther we went from Petrograd the quieter the country became. Then we left all trouble behind and the train speeded on in what seemed a peaceful and happy land.

At last we reached Christiania and there I found kind friends. They gave me the first really satisfying food I had had in many days. In addition they gave me kindness and the quiet of their home. While awaiting word from the United States, I rested and won back some measure of my strength.

More funds reached me at Christiania, and I soon found myself aboard an ocean liner bound for Halifax, on my way to the land of freedom. From Halifax I came direct to New York. As the Statue of Liberty was pointed out to me as we entered the harbor, I rejoiced not merely because I, myself, was safe at last, but because I had at last reached the country where I was to deliver the message that would bring help to my suffering people.

Here I found good friends — kindly Americans who have made me as happy as ever I can be. And, best of all, they are not being kind merely to one unfortunate girl — they are sending help to those I left behind — to those who are still alive and lost in the sandy deserts. They have made it possible for me to tell in this, my book, what General Andranik said to me:

"Armenia is trusting to her friends — the people of the United States."

*

Map showing Aurora's wanderings

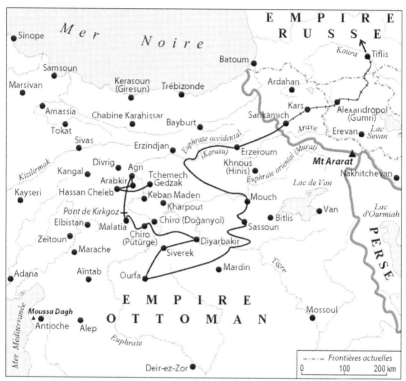

© Eric Van Lauwe

Contents

My dedication 5

Acknowledgment 6

Foreword..7

ARSHALUS - THE LIGHT OF THE MORNING 13

I WHEN THE PASHA CAME TO MY HOUSE 19

II THE DAYS OF TERROR BEGIN...................................30

III VAHBY BEY TAKES HIS CHOICE 41

IV THE CRUEL SMILE OF KEMAL EFFENDI 50

V THE WAYS OF THE ZAPTIEHS....................................62

VI RECRUITING FOR THE HAREMS OF CONSTANTINOPLE 73

VII MALATIA — THE CITY OF DEATH 83

VIII IN THE HAREM OF HADJI GHAFOUR 92

IX THE RAID ON THE MONASTERY 101

X THE GAME OF THE SWORDS, AND DIYARBEKIR 112

XI "ISHIM YOK; KEIFIM TCHOK!" 123

XII REUNION — AND THEN, THE SHEIKH ZILAN 134

XIII OLD VARTABED AND THE SHEPHERD'S CALL 144

XIV THE MESSAGE OF GENERAL ANDRANIK.........................155

Map showing Aurora's wanderings..............................165

Made in United States
North Haven, CT
03 December 2023

44940306R00102